The Cybrarian's Guide to Developing Successful Internet Programs and Services

Diane and Michael Kovacs

NEAL-SCHUMAN NETGUIDE SERIES

Neal-Schuman Publishers, Inc.

New York   London

Published by Neal-Schuman Publishers
100 Varick Street
New York, NY 10013

Library of Congress Cataloging-in-Publication Data

Kovacs, Michael.
    The cybrarian's guide for developing successful Internet programs and services / by Michael and Diane Kovacs.
        p.   cm.
    Includes bibliographical references and index.
    ISBN 1-55570-287-2
    1. Library information networks—United States. 2. Library information networks. 3. Internet (Computer network)—United States. 4. Internet (Computer network) 5. Electronic publishing—United States. 6. Electronic publishing. I. Kovacs, Diane. II. Title
Z674.75.I58K68   1997
025.04—dc21   96-37750

Contents

List of Figures

Preface

The Cybrarian's Guide to Developing Successful Internet Programs and Services is written for librarians who are already very familiar with the Internet as advanced endusers; this book is not for beginning Internet users. Beginners should instead refer to such books as *The Complete Internet Companion for Librarians*, by Allen C. Benson, and *The Internet Complete Reference*, 2d. ed., by Harley Hahn.

Advanced endusers—as assumed in this book—are individuals who know basically how the TCP/IP software and telecommunications infrastructure works to create the Internet. They also know the basics of Internet domain-name addressing, and have extensive experience using all Internet services, including

- E-mail—Advanced end users have used e-mail for interpersonal and discussion list interaction. They have subscribed to e-mail–based discussions (managed by Listserv, Listproc, Majordomo and the like) and have set options for those discussions. It will be helpful if they have also searched discussion list archives through e-mail.
- FTP—Advanced endusers have FTPed software and graphics as well as simple text files. They also understand how to interpret file extensions such as .zip, .hqx, .tar, .gif in terms of what kind of files they are and how to work with them.
- Telnet—Advanced endusers have frequently telneted to sites all over the world. As a result, they understand the diversity of user interfaces that are encountered through telnet connections.
- Gopher—Advanced endusers have used Gopher and have a clear idea of what kinds of resources are stored in or linked to by Gopher servers. They understand the Gopher addressing systems. Most importantly, they understand the client-server relationship that is essential to Gopher as well as World Wide Web connections through the Internet.

- World Wide Web—Advanced endusers have used the World Wide Web (Web) and have created at least one simple Web page. They know the basics of HTML markup (forms, frames, and CGI or Java programs are *not* basic). It is especially important that they understand the use and purpose of the URL (Universal Resource Locator) format and the client-server relationships that make the World Wide Web possible on the Internet.

After reading *The Cybrarian's Guide to Developing Successful Internet Programs and Services* you will be prepared to use the Internet as a publication and information dissemination tool. You will be prepared to become an Internet information producer and/or provider. For example, you will be able to plan, implement, and maintain a local library Web site as an electronic library; you will be able to plan, implement, and maintain an electronic journal or newsletter; you might even use the Internet to provide distance education.

The focus of this book is on planning, creating, and maintaining advanced Internet applications. The term "application" as used in this book means the information product created. Internet services are not the applications that we're concerned with, rather they are merely the tools that can be used to create and distribute the information products. The Internet is an international computer network that uses the TCP/IP software and telecommunications infrastructure to create connections between computers. The services that the existence of the Internet makes possible (e-mail, FTP, Gopher, and World Wide Web, for example) are distribution and communication tools. The World Wide Web is currently the most "advanced" Internet service, since it allows high-speed connections, interactivity, and efficient graphics transfer. But, in fact, many excellent information products are created and distributed using the more basic Internet services, especially e-mail.

An Internet application may also be a service provided through personal contact rather than an information product distributed through the Internet. For example, your library might choose to offer Internet training, or even technical support and software recommendations to endusers.

We wrote this book as a culmination of six years of consulting with clients and students who wanted to become Internet information producers and/or providers, as well as from our own experiences in being Internet information producers and providers.

HOW THIS BOOK IS ORGANIZED

Chapter 1 is required reading for anyone using this book, as it lays the foundation for the remaining chapters. This chapter is about why and how to become an Internet information producer or provider; it outlines the basic and ideal Internet connectivity and computer platforms required to provide information effectively through the Internet, how to choose appropriate Internet distribution mechanisms for your information product; and how to plan for the time, personnel—and training—required to create and maintain an Internet information product.

Chapters 2 through 6 follow a common format:

- Planning issues—Writing a project plan, assessing equipment and software needs, staffing, and training.
- Implementation—Getting to work creating the Internet application.
- Maintenance—Staffing issues, upgrades, and expansions.
- Case description(s)—Sidebars with real-life examples of advanced Internet applications. These are used to illustrate points in the planning, implementation, and maintenance sections.

Chapter 2 is specifically about designing Internet training programs. This chapter also examines the planning, creation, and maintenance of distance education projects through the Internet. The L.O.S.T. project to provide Internet training for librarians without access to other training opportunities is highlighted.

Chapter 3 discusses several real projects for offering and marketing traditional library services through the Internet. It includes examples from public and corporate as well as academic libraries. For example, Kitsap Regional Library in Washington state is providing access to the Internet and promoting library services to its public through the Internet.

Chapter 4 discusses the planning, creation, and maintenance of electronic libraries. The Cleveland Public Libraries' electronic library project is used as an example of a general electronic library. Purdue University's government documents project is used as an example of a specialized electronic library.

Chapter 5 discusses electronic journal and newsletter production and distribution, and archiving projects. *PACS Review*, one of the first and best e-journals, and *IAT Infobits*, one of the first and best e-newsletters, are highlighted.

Chapter 6 is a concluding discussion of beginning and continuing Internet information products and of one more kind of information product.

Appendix A lists selected freeware, shareware, and commercial Internet services software and describes where to retrieve the software.

Appendix B is an annotated directory of URLs that link to selected Internet tutorials and FAQs for setting up Internet services (e-mail distributions, FTP, Gopher, and World Wide Web) on selected platforms. These are not enduser tutorials, but are intended for the person who will be responsible for installing and maintaining Internet services software.

Appendix C is a tutorial called "Just Enough Unix." It is meant to give non-computer professionals enough knowledge of Unix to install their own Web pages or to use a Unix account to manage an e-mail distribution form. Note that Internet server software requires root access to install and maintain—that means a Unix system administrator is required.

Appendix D is a list of discussion lists and newsgroups for Internet information producers and providers. It includes discussion lists and newsgroups where you can discuss your plans with others who are also interested in creating Internet applications.

An annotated bibliography of print resources is provided in Appendix E.

COMPUTER PLATFORMS AND LIBRARY APPLICATIONS

We focus on practical applications, realistic implementations, and recommend software and computer platforms that are accessible to non-computer systems professionals.

The Windows, Unix, and Power Macintosh platforms are equitably addressed throughout this book. Windows Internet services software is easily available and inexpensive. Craig Hunt has written a book, *Networking Personal Computers with TCP/IP*, which provides detailed instructions. The Windows NT Internet server platform is very powerful. It has some of the ease of the Macintosh platform with much of the power of the Unix platform. One drawback is that Microsoft may force those wishing to use Windows NT as a Internet Server to use the Windows NT Advanced Server

(NTAS), because Microsoft is restricting the number of Web connections possible on machines running Windows NT.

The Unix operating system, Unix Internet services software, and a good high-speed Unix computer system are the best platform on which to implement advanced Internet applications that are meant for regional, national, or international access. Unix is especially appropriate because it is the best inexpensive multi-tasking computer operating system available. Linux is a version of Unix which runs on Intel-based microcomputers. It is inexpensive, as are the Intel-based microcomputers. Such a system absolutely requires a skilled system administrator in addition to the people planning, creating, and maintaining applications on the system. Several books on establishing Internet connections on Unix platforms are listed in Appendix E.

The Power Macintosh software and computer platform is our favorite because setting up Internet services is so easy. Rarely would a computer professional be required to assist librarians establishing advanced Internet applications using Power Macintosh. You'll need to know the IP address assigned to you by your Internet service provider or network systems administrator and where to type it in.

One principle that is continuously stressed is the requirement that skilled computer systems people be available or hired when needed. Librarians tend to be extraordinarily intelligent and capable individuals, but some activities require us to collaborate with skilled professionals in other disciplines. We do mean collaborate. We've worked with librarians who say to us that "the computer services guys won't work with us" or "the computer center won't help." Further inquiry usually reveals that the librarians didn't "ask"; they assumed the computer services staff could read their minds and the librarians did not make clear what they wanted to do and why. Sometimes the computer services staff will not be willing to work with you. In such cases have your administration talk to their administration about collaboration between your departments. Remember, the "computer center people" are professionals too.

The Internet application case studies are included with the permission of the librarians responsible for them. All of these folks have given us permission to include their name and e-mail address and their library's name. In Chapter 3, the descriptions were provided by the contributors. In the other chapters the descriptions are based on responses that contributors made to e-mailed questionnaires. They have also had the opportunity to read through these case descriptions. However, we are responsible for any errors in description.

We hope that you'll use this book as a starting point to get to work on your own Internet applications. If you have questions please feel free to e-mail us at diane@kovacs.com or michael@kovacs.com.

Chapter 1

Why and How to Become an Internet Information Producer or Provider (IIPOP)

BECOMING AN IIPOP

The three basic phases to becoming an Internet Information Producer or Provider (IIPOP) are planning, implementation, and maintenance.

This chapter focuses on the first step, planning. We strongly advise you to create a written plan. A written plan can help a group of implementors focus on the nitty-gritty details of implementation and maintenance, and help convince administrators to fund or otherwise support the project. There are some clear steps to producing a planning document. The order is not important; the order in this book reflects our personal strategy for approaching planning to become an IIPOP. Figure 1.1 outlines some questions you'll need to answer while planning to become an IIPOP.

Why Should You or Your Library Become an IIPOP?

Almost inevitably you will have to answer this question if you want support from your library's administration for your project. It is not good enough to say either "Because everyone is doing it" or "Be-

---

Figure 1.1 Questions to Ask in Planning Internet Applications

1. Why should you or your library want to become an Internet Information Producer or Provider?

2. For whom are you providing the information product? What kind of Internet connectivity is available to them? Does your site already have an appropriate level of Internet connectivity?

3. What kind of information product will you provide? Why is it an important and/ or appropriate information product for your library, school, company, or organization to provide?

4. Do you have personnel who are knowledgeable enough to produce and maintain such an information product? How many people will be needed to start up and maintain the project?

5. What Internet distribution mechanism(s) will you use? Why? (Such mechanisms are sometimes dictated by available computer hardware and software and by funding availability.)

6. What computer hardware and software is already available to you through your library, company, or organization? What computer hardware and software will you need to purchase or otherwise acquire?

7. What kind of security is in place? What level of security will you need?

8. How much time do you estimate the project will take to start up and then maintain?

---

cause it's neat." The answer to this question requires careful thought. There are a number of good reasons why your library would benefit from becoming an IIPOP:

- Your library can generate good publicity among endusers. This is especially important for universities where many prospective students and faculty are checking out colleges and universities through their Web pages.
- Your library can create and maintain an image and reality of innovative thinking and activity among library professionals. In other words, you can use your Internet presence to attract quality personnel, grants, and even awards.
- Your library can make it easier for endusers to access important Internet and traditional resources on-site (for example, FirstSearch, Wilson, and SilverPlatter databases).

Such access could be especially valuable in the very busy or understaffed library.

- Your library can provide many traditional library services to off-site endusers. Remote access is especially useful for business libraries that serve multiple corporate sites and for colleges and universities with commuter students or branch campuses.
- Your library can move human resources from maintaining paper and CD-ROM resources to providing networked services.

You may choose any or all of the above to justify becoming an IIPOP. We're sure there are other good reasons as well. (If you'd like to share yours, please e-mail them to us at diane@kovacs.com.)

Decisions made in this first step are heavily dependent on who your intended audience is. Do you want to provide information for your colleagues in the profession? for staff of your library? for end users at your library, school, business, or organization? for faculty, staff, or students at your school? for the general public regionally, nationally, or internationally?

For whom are you providing the information product? What kind of Internet connectivity is available to them? Does your site already have an appropriate level of Internet connectivity?

Your community of endusers or the people you would like to become your endusers are a key factor in any decisions you make. If your endusers aren't likely to have a particular level of Internet connectivity (for example, the graphics capability required for good World Wide Web resources), then it doesn't make sense to provide highly graphical information through that mechanism. You may need to plan for basic, text-only access.

It may seem obvious to you that to become an Internet information provider you must be connected to the Internet. Believe it or not, we have worked with students and clients who began planning Internet information products without first checking to see if they had an adequate Internet connection available to them. You must have at least one computer directly connected to the Internet in order to run Internet services through it. An Internet service is what the Internet experts call the things we know as e-mail, FTP, telnet, Gopher, and the World Wide Web. They are computer software products that work on top of the TCP/IP software to allow different levels or kinds of access to and between other computers on the Internet.

Your next decision will probably be the basis of most of the other decisions you make involving your Internet connection: the type and speed of your connection. Your choice will depend on how much bandwidth you need and how much you can afford.

Most Internet access providers offer the following connection options:

- Point to Point Protocol (PPP) or Serial Line Internet Protocol (SLIP) 14,400–28,800 bps dial-up connection
- 56k or 64k bps Frame Relay
- 56k or 64k Digital Data Service (DDS)
- 64k or 128k bps ISDN-PPP
- other T1-based frame relay and DDS services

The problem with dial-up connections is that you are converting digital signals to cross over analog phone lines and then converting them back into digital signals at the other end. This slows things down considerably. This is the least expensive option for Internet access. Most value-added Internet providers can give cheap PPP (or SLIP) connections.

A 56k or 64k bps Frame Relay uses existing digital telephone lines or public data lines. These work similarly to the older X.25 public data networks (such as Tymnet, Telenet, Sprintnet) but they can sustain higher connection speeds than the slower X.25 standard (around 19.2k bps top sustained speed for X.25, 38.4k bps for Frame Relay) while the cost is much the same. This type of connection is available through many telephone companies including MCI, Ameritech, and AT&T. Many regional telephone companies are also able to make Frame Relay available.

A 56k or 64k Digital Data Service (DDS) dedicated line connected directly to your Internet provider provides optimum performance and bandwidth for most companies. This kind of connection is usually available only through the regional Internet providers or telephone companies. The hardware necessary for a DDS connection will cost from $1,500 to $2,000.

A 64k or 128k bps ISDN-PPP connection is the next step up in performance. Where good standardized ISDN is available, ISDN can provide up to 128k throughput. An ISDN terminal adapter is required for an ISDN connection. The ISDN connection is plugged into the adaptor on one end and into the network router on the other. There are also boxes available that serve as the IP Router for a network. You can expect to pay up to $1,500 for a good ISDN bridge-router.

T1 lines are the next step up, with bandwidth of 1.4 Meg/second throughput. Fractional T1 lines are available for lesser cost. This option is expensive but probably necessary for anyone wanting to provide an Internet Information Product to the entire international Internet community or even to a very large group of regional endusers. The cost for a T1 line connection is at least $12,000 per year.

With any of these connections you can run your own Internet servers to provide FTP, telnet, Gopher, or World Wide Web services. Once you start allowing two-way connections, however, security may become a major issue for your library. You should discuss these issues with your provider or an independent expert.

With the exception of manually managed e-mail distributions, dial-up SLIP or PPP connections simply do not provide the data transfer speed required for offering Internet services. Furthermore, the two-way connectivity requires that the SLIP or PPP connection be constantly connected. The minimal Internet connectivity recommended for an IIPOP is either a 56k dedicated line or a single-channel (64k) ISDN connection. Most colleges and universities already have much higher speed Internet connectivity available to them. Schools, organizations, and businesses may or may not have a high level of connectivity. We recommend that you find a good Internet provider in your area and possibly a good Internet consultant. If you need recommendations ask other people who have used such services. If you have e-mail (anyone can get basic one-way Internet access through America Online, CompuServe, or similar services), you can join discussion groups and ask the people who participate for their recommendations. For university and college librarians, Libref-L or Web4Lib are usually very productive. School librarians will find much good interaction through LM_Net. Business librarians will find Buslib-L to be an excellent resource. Subscription instructions for these groups are provided in Appendix D. Karen Schneider's awesome *Internet Access Cookbook* is a very intelligent description of how to evaluate, access, and set up the technology you'll need. An excellent book for evaluating and establishing Internet connections of 56k bps and up is Kevin Dowd's *Getting Connected: The Internet at 56K and Up.*

What kind of information product will you provide? Why is it an important and/or appropriate information product for your library, school, company, or organization to provide?

Once you've decided who your audience is and what the justification for your information product is, then it's time to decide what form your information product will take. The following list is representative of the majority of information products made available through the Internet by libraries:

- Internet training programs and distance education
- traditional library resources and services
- electronic journals and electronic newsletters
- electronic libraries

Internet training programs are a valuable service that libraries can provide for endusers and local library staff. As you will read in Chapter 2, the Internet is also an excellent vehicle through which to provide distance education to the general library profession or other constituency. Some library schools have even begun offering classes through the Internet—the University of Illinois at Urbana-Champaign's Graduate School of Library and Information Science, offers selected classes through the Internet (more information is available at http://alexia.lis.uiuc.edu/leep3/).

Offering or marketing traditional library services through the Internet may be as simple as providing a gateway to the library catalog, and to text and graphics that describe library services. Marketing can also include providing valuable library research services through e-mail. In Chapter 3, we highlight several excellent, real-life marketing projects. In fact, putting any information product on the Internet has the effect of marketing library services.

Electronic libraries are becoming more and more common. Typically they provide as many library services (including catalogs, commercial or locally produced databases, and reference assistance) as the physical library. Of course there is nothing like the face-to-face research assistance that librarians can provide in person, but e-mail and answers to frequently asked questions (FAQs) about the library can do a pretty good job for many endusers. In Chapter 4, a comprehensive electronic library project and a special electronic library project are described.

Electronic journals and electronic newsletters can substitute for similar print information products. In fact, it is becoming more likely that your endusers will read an e-mailed electronic newsletter than one you send through postal or campus mail, and its production and distribution will be much less expensive. In terms of providing an information product for the general public or the library profession as a whole, the "e-journal" is very profitable. The overhead for the intellectual contribution to an e-journal is similar to that for producing a print journal, especially in terms of human time. Production and distribution costs, however, are very small. This means that any library or library school with sufficient personnel to support the project and with basic Internet connectivity can produce an e-journal. The Library of Congress catalogs and assigns International Standard Serial Numbers (ISSNs) to e-journals through the same process that it provides ISSNs to print journals.

Do you have personnel who are knowledgeable enough to produce and maintain such an information product? How many people will be needed to start up and maintain the project?

Just about anyone with advanced Internet knowledge can create an application distributable through an Internet service. In fact, many libraries have depended on library school or other graduate students to create and maintain Internet applications conceived and designed by library staff. Depending on the platform you choose you may need a system administrator who will install and maintain Internet services for you.

Some general rules of thumb when planning for staffing are described below. In subsequent chapters more specific staffing issues are addressed.

- Plan for learning and training time—no matter how much you or your colleagues know, you'll always need time to read the directions or explore options. Even experienced computer systems administrators need time to learn new things. We recommend planning your time and then doubling it to accommodate learning and training time.
- Internet information products take as much intellectual, edi-

torial, and clerical working time to create and maintain as other information products. The e-newsletter or e-journal must be written and edited, the database must be compiled and indexed, the training program must be developed and presented, the reference question must be analyzed, researched, and answered. The distribution phase is the phase where time and/or money may be saved using the Internet versus other mechanisms.

- Enthusiasm, seniority, or titles do not necessarily ensure that an individual is knowledgeable enough to create an information product—Internet or otherwise. Think critically in designating yourself or others to work on the project. We often turn to colleagues with better knowledge for help with our projects. One of the most helpful colleagues we ever worked with was an 8-year-old (he trained Diane to use Diversity University MOO)! Library staff and graduate students are frequently excellent staffing choices. After all, how many libraries' newsletters are actually produced by a secretary?

What Internet distribution mechanism(s) will you use? Why?

The answers to this question depend on the answer to the question "What information product am I producing and providing?" If you are creating a database that must be both constantly updated and permanently archived, you would not want to use e-mail or FTP distributions. If you are producing a current e-newsletter or e-journal, however, you would want to consider those options. The Internet services available at this writing and their strengths in terms of different information product distributions are described below. These options are not mutually exclusive—in fact many information products are distributed through multiple Internet distribution mechanisms.

E-mail. E-mail is the ideal Internet distribution option for a number of information products. Personalized e-mail reference services or strategic dissemination of information services are simple for both the librarian and the enduser. E-mail can be sent through a Web page so that all a library's services can be offered in a one-stop location. For example, in Chapter 3 there is a case description of Indiana University Libraries' Web page, through which they offer their "Ask a Librarian" service. Endusers type their e-mail address and their question into a Web form. Librarians then read the messages and reply through e-mail.

E-mail is also a reasonable mechanism for distributing e-journals or e-newsletters. L-Soft Listserv, Listproc, and Majordomo are the three major kinds of software for managing subscriber lists and other functions for discussion groups or e-serials through e-mail. There are several other good programs (for example, Mailbase, United Kingdom only; Comserve, through Rennselaer Polytechnic Institute only) which you might have available locally, but in this book we focus on the major three.

FTP. FTP servers allow storage and access for copying files from a remote Internet-connected computer. FTP is best used for archiving information. It's a good way to provide access to back issues of e-journals or e-newsletters for subscribers who may not have Gopher or Web access.

Telnet. Telnet is not in and of itself an Internet distribution service. It is a tool for connecting to stored databases or interactive services on remote computers. Telnet allows Internet-connected computers to connect to each other and for the connecting computer to use services available on the remote computer. Those services and databases can be quite unique and have many different commands for interaction. Telnet used to be the connection mechanism of choice for real-time interactive access to large databases through the Internet; most library catalogs are telnet accessible. Telnet is also used for making real-time connections to text-based virtual reality systems like Diversity University (which is discussed in Chapter 2). Telnet connections are continuous—that is, the enduser's computer is connected throughout the interaction with the remote computer. Telnet server software creates "ports" to which each connection is made. There is a limit to the number of ports based on the telnet server and the platform on which it is installed. No one else can connect to an occupied port until the enduser logs off. This continuous connection can make telnet an inefficient choice for sites with less powerful computer platforms or for access to very popular resources. While telnet is still useful for real-time connections, access to databases can be done more easily and more efficiently through Gopher or World Wide Web servers. Gopher and World Wide Web servers offer uniform enduser interfaces as well.

Security of the system can also be a very high concern with telnet connections as the connection might allow knowledgeable crackers to access critical areas of telnet-accessible computers. The kinds of services offered through telnet connections have proved to be especially vulnerable.

Gopher. Gopher was the first alternative to telnet for real-time interactive access to information on the Internet.

The Gopher service has three different parts: the Gopher connection, the Gopher server, and the Gopher client. The Gopher connection is similar to an FTP connection, except that Gopher client software connects specifically to a Gopher server. The client retrieves information from the Gopher server and brings it back to the enduser's computer and then disconnects. The port is thus freed up and another enduser can connect.

Gopher clients are available for all common computer platforms. All of these are easy for anyone with enduser knowledge of his or her computer platform to install and use.

Gopher servers are also available for all common computer platforms and in most cases are very easy to set up. Usually, all that is required is knowledge of creating directories and editing files on the chosen computer platform. In addition to providing real-time access to databases on a host machine, Gopher allows a variety of information products to be organized in a logical hierarchical manner by any person with basic computer skills for the platform on which the Gopher server is running.

A Gopher server allows IIPOPs to create links to other Gopher servers, telnet sites, and FTP sites as well as to locally stored text files. Gopher-related programs are available that allow keyword and boolean searching of text files stored on the Gopher server. There is also a "Gopherspace" (all registered Gopher servers on the Internet) search tool called Veronica. Veronica allows endusers to search for directories and files stored on Gopher servers. Gopher was a major step forward in allowing IIPOPs to use the Internet for enduser services. Previously, mechanisms for organizing resources on the Internet required someone with strong programming skills as well as thorough knowledge of the TCP/IP protocols. It is still very useful for IIPOPs and their endusers who do not have World Wide Web access (for example, those who have e-mail service only).

World Wide Web. The World Wide Web allows archiving and interactive retrieval of text, graphics, sound, and video. World Wide Web servers can be used to transact commerce securely through the Internet, with an appropriate Web client (such as Netscape).

Like Gopher, the World Wide Web has three parts: the HTTP (hypertext transport protocol) connection, Web clients, and Web servers. The HTTP connection is the same kind of connection as the Gopher connection—that is, it opens a connection from the client to the server, requests information from the server, and the client receives the information and then closes the connection. The difference is that HTTP is MIME-compliant; it allows for the transfer of many more types of information, including graphics, video, and sound, and even allows Web clients to request that a server run a program and send the output back to the client (CGI programs). MIME is a Multimedia Internet Mail Extension, originally a standard for sending different types of information through Internet e-mail. Now it is a general standard for identifying the contents of information being passed across the Internet via HTTP.

World Wide Web clients have proliferated in the past three years. Like Gopher, there are both text-only and graphical Web clients. The text-only client most commonly used is Lynx which runs on the Unix, VAX/VMS, and DOS platforms. NCSA Mosaic, created by the University of Illinois National Center for Super Computer Applications was the first graphical client programmed for a consumer-grade microcomputer. It was initially programmed for the Apple Macintosh platform, which at that time it was generally the only consumer microcomputer capable of displaying both graphics and sound. Later versions were created for the Unix X-Windows and Microsoft Windows platform. Netscape is a commercial graphical Web client created by some of the people who created Mosaic. Netscape is in our opinion the best Web client available now and in the foreseeable future. Netscape and Mosaic are available for Unix workstation, Macintosh, and Windows platforms. The Web client software's capabilities, combined with the capabilities of the computer platform that it runs on, is what determines whether endusers can see graphics, hear sound, or view videos on their system. Macintoshes and Unix workstations have sound and video built in. Windows microcomputers may or may not come with sound and video built in, but they are increasingly so equipped. These functions also require that the user have installed "helper" applications (such as SoundMachine or MovieMachine) that can be launched by the Web client software in order to generate sound or video.

Microsoft also includes a Web browser (called Internet Explorer) with recent versions of Windows, Windows 95, and Windows NT.

World Wide Web servers are available for every computer platform. Appendix A lists some of the free and shareware versions and provides access instructions. Commercial World Wide Web servers range in cost from around $200 for a basic server to around $50,000 for a powerful security server suitable for banking or other financial transactions.

What computer hardware and software is already available to you through your library, company, or organization? What computer hardware and software will you need to purchase or otherwise acquire?

This is really a matter of inventorying what you have. If you lack what you need then read the rest of this section.

If this section doesn't make sense to you, you are probably not ready to start creating advanced Internet applications. You can learn what you need to know relatively quickly. The best way is to find a knowledgeable person, collaborate with that person and learn from him or her. You can find people willing to help in your own computer services department or through one of the recommended discussion groups.

In case you don't already know, a platform is a computer hardware and operating system combination. If a particular platform is already in use in your library, you'll first need to talk to the systems people at your site to find out what kind of computers and operating systems they are using. If you are supposed to decide what kind of platform to purchase, then you might want either to take our advice or to contact an Internet consultant in your area. If you work with a consultant, it is best to ask if the consultant has a relationship or vested interest in the platforms sold by a particular company. We've met a few consultants who are really resellers who will only recommend their product, whether appropriate or not.

The platform for Internet applications can be anything from a high-speed Unix workstation (any brand, but Hewlett Packard or Digital Equipment Corporation's Alpha workstations seem to have the best price/performance ratio) to an Internet-connected microcomputer running MS Windows. The very best platform is any Unix system running the Internet services software available for Unix.

This option can be expensive because you will need to have available or hire someone with Unix systems expertise, at least during the start-up phase.

If you have a Macintosh that is Internet connected you are in very good shape. It is our opinion that the Apple Power Macintoshes running the appropriate Internet services software are the best platform to use when there are no computer professionals available. The Power Macs are also very powerful and relatively inexpensive compared to other adequate platforms. They are designed with Internet and other networking options in mind. The Internet services software programs available for Macintosh are exquisitely easy to set up and use. For example, to set up the Web server software MacHTTP (see Appendix A), FTP the MacHTTP software to your Internet-connected Mac, then simply double-click on the icon for the program. You are now running a very good Web server and can associate Web pages with it simply by storing the HTML documents in the same folder as the MacHTTP software. Your Web server's homepage must be named default.html.

If you have an IBM/VM/CMS mainframe you will need to have the full cooperation of your IBM/VM/CMS systems people. You can run e-mail, FTP, telnet, and Gopher servers on an IBM mainframe. Recently a decent World Wide Web server for IBM mainframes (Webshare—see Appendix A) was developed. However, the text-based World Wide Web client that is available for the IBM mainframe is not pleasant to use (it is not the same as Lynx, which runs on Unix, DOS, and VMS platforms). Setting up an FTP service on an IBM mainframe is also very complex. In terms of e-mail, however, the IBM mainframe is good. The L-Soft Listserv (formerly Bitnet Listserv) software was originally programmed for the IBM/VM/CMS, although it is now available for many other platforms on the Internet, including VMS, Windows NT, and many varieties of Unix.

VAX/VMS platform is almost as nice as the Unix platform. Again, you must have a good working arrangement with the VAX/VMS systems managers in order to install and maintain any server software that you want to use. VMS e-mail is not easy to use, but the FTP and telnet server software programs are good. There are also excellent Gopher and World Wide Web server software programs as well as text-only client software for the VAX/VMS platform.

It is possible to run Internet services from Microsoft Windows PCs, but it is very complex and the servers are prone to performance problems. Microsoft also produces Windows NT, an operating system for PCs that solves many of the problems with using machines running the previous versions of Windows as Internet servers. Windows NT is relatively expensive but it is a fine Internet server platform. Many people who want to use a PC install Linux, a freeware Unix operating system software program for PCs, instead of Windows. In that case they are simply using what computer professionals call an "Intel Box" to run the Unix operating system. This is a good plan if you have 486s or Pentiums (Intel Boxes) already available. You'll still need skilled Unix system administrators but you won't have to pay for a high-speed Unix workstation.

What kind of security is in place? What level of security will you need?

Running a Web server is not inherently insecure, but being connected to the Internet and running Internet services is. If you are running only clients then you are safe. The best strategy when running Internet servers of any kind is to put them on computers that are dedicated to that purpose. If you're using existing computers they may have other sensitive data that you might want to protect, for example patron circulation or library financial records.

The basic security is password protection and file permissions. Basic security is part of your computer's operating system and usually this will be enough. There are ways around this basic security, however. IP spoofing, where a cracker can use software to make his or her computer appear to be on your local network, is one example. More commonly a cracker will simply exploit known bugs in the security of your operating system.

If you want to secure more thoroughly against attempted computer break-ins and possible vandalism, you may want to think about Firewall software for your network. A Firewall gives you very strong control over the network traffic passing in and out of your site. A Firewall is a separate computer running special software that monitors all incoming—and, if desired, all outgoing—network traffic. You can configure the Firewall to restrict access to particular domains, particular types of Internet connections, and much more.

The World Wide Web Security FAQ (http://www-genome.wi. mit.edu/WWW/faqs/www-security-faq.html) answers many questions that you might have about network security for your Web server.

How much time do you estimate the project will take to start up and then maintain?

The answer to this question will really depend on what kind of Internet information product you choose. Subsequent chapters will give you some ideas about time requirements.

GENERAL INTERNET APPLICATION DESIGN ISSUES

There are probably as many ways to design information presentation as there are people in the world. Following are general guidelines that will make your Internet information product more accessible and usable:

- Diversify Internet access to your information product.
- Use ASCII text as your standard text format. HTML uses ASCII text for both the content and the format information.
- Keep your information product simple and uncluttered.
- Plan for archiving your information product.

Diversify Internet Access to Your Information Product

There is justification for diversifying Internet distribution mechanisms. Many endusers will have e-mail but will not have access to other Internet services. Others may have only a World Wide Web client. Especially in the developing countries and the newly independent former Soviet republics, endusers have very basic Internet connections. Information providers who want to maximize access to their publication will be sensitive to the variety of Internet connections of potential information users.

Use ASCII Text as Your Standard Text Format

The World Wide Web bases HTML coding on ASCII text for a very good reason. ASCII text is an international standard format for text. Any word processor, or text browser, text editor, or viewer can open and display an ASCII text file. Other formats are also used on the Internet, including Postscript, which requires endusers to have a Postscript interpreter installed on their computer or to have a Postscript printer available, and Adobe Acrobat, which requires users to have the Adobe Acrobat reader installed. Postscript, in our opinion, is not a good choice for formatting text on the Internet unless your audience is limited to those with Postscript interpreters installed. Adobe Acrobat format is nice if you can assume that your users will have the Adobe Acrobat reader available to them. It's also conceivable that you will be producing an information product only for a very specific group (for example, Macintosh users or Microsoft Word users); in those cases you can provide your information product in a more specific format (such as unencoded or binhexed Microsoft Word documents).

Keep Your Information Product Simple and Uncluttered

Complex search systems or involved login procedures will baffle many endusers. Many otherwise valuable Internet databases are little used because they are so difficult to use. An example is E.T.Net, a health science, educational technology bulletin board run by the National Library of Medicine (telnet://etnet.nlm.nih.gov:login etnet). A nursing professor who evaluated it as part of an advanced Internet workshop said it was a wonderful idea but so difficult to connect to and so complex to navigate that she would not use it again or recommend it to others.

Pictures, variable fonts, and other graphical presentations including color are available as part of information products distributed through the World Wide Web. Keep pictures, fonts, and colors simple and few; endusers who have text-only Web clients will not be able to see them anyway. Endusers with slow connections (SLIP or PPP) are the majority of Web users right now, and the time it takes to display complex and numerous graphics can be frustrating to them. A Web page should communicate effectively in both text-only and graphical clients.

Plan for Archiving Your Information Product

The permanency of Internet information products has been discussed and rediscussed since the potential for archiving on the Internet was first conceived. FTP servers were the original Internet archives. Files stored on FTP servers include graphics and software, as well as ASCII text. The information is stored on disks on the computer system at the FTP site and will stay there safely unless someone deletes it, or until there is a disk crash and data is corrupted. As with any electronic archiving mechanism, frequent backups of the information are required to keep it safe. Information products can be archived on the Internet through mailing list fileservers (for example, Listserv) and FTP servers as well as Gophers and Web sites.

One should diversify archiving mechanisms for the same reasons that one should diversify distribution mechanisms. An information product that we produce was once accidentally lost from the FTP site where it was archived. This was not a serious loss because copies on Gophers and Web sites were easily obtained to replace the lost FTP site archives.

SUMMARY

In deciding to become an IIPOP, you'll need to consider carefully why you want to produce and provide information through the Internet, as well as how you're going to do it. Deciding what application to create and whether you've got appropriate staff to produce and maintain it is the next step. Ensuring that you have an adequate Internet connection through which to offer your Internet application is a priority.

Choosing which Internet services software to use is simple as each has different functions. Which version or brand to use can be an issue. The best strategy is to ask others who have already created projects what they did and how they feel about the software they chose.

The choices of computer platforms are diverse and may depend on what you already have available or what you can afford.

The following chapters offer more detailed strategies for developing different Internet applications and they relate experiences of other IIPOPs.

Chapter 2

Internet Training and Distance Education Through the Internet

Many libraries are finding that, either because of demands from their user community or because of state or regional legislation, they have no choice but to provide Internet training to their endusers as well as to their staff. In many states public and school libraries are receiving mandates to introduce the Internet into their service repertoire. Businesses around the world are turning to the Internet as a tool for communicating and for marketing; business librarians are often expected to lead the way. As they are discovering, the Internet itself is a great mechanism through which to provide training.

This chapter deals with the planning, implementation, and maintenance of Internet training (both in the classroom and through the Internet) and covers the use of the Internet as a distance education tool. Case descriptions of librarians providing Internet training in the classroom and through the Internet are used to illustrate the discussion. Complete case descriptions are located as sidebars within the chapter.

Figure 2.1   Questions to Ask in Planning for Internet Training

1. What training facilities are available? Do you have demonstration capabilities or a lab with Internet connected computers?

2. What level and kind of Internet training will you provide? Hands-on or demonstration only? Will you teach how to use a Web client? Will you access one particular site or cover everything from e-mail to Webcrawler and how to build a Web page?

3. For whom are you providing the Internet training? Students? Faculty? Library staff? Endusers? The general public? The whole world?

4. Do you or your colleagues have the necessary knowledge to provide good, accurate Internet training at the level you've chosen?

5. What Internet services will you teach? Why?

6. What kind of promotion will you have for the training? E-mail announcements? Flyers through "snail mail"? A notice at the start-up screen on your system or on your Web page or Gopher server? Posters in your building and other buildings at your site?

7. How much time do you estimate it will take to design the training, including the development of training materials?

8. How much time will you have to teach each session, and how will you schedule the sessions?

9. How many people will be needed to provide the training?

10. What mechanisms will you use to evaluate the effectiveness of the training?

PLANNING

Internet training programs present some unique issues that must be considered. Figure 2.1 outlines the issues discussed in this chapter.

WHAT TRAINING FACILITIES ARE AVAILABLE?

Demonstration capabilities, that is a microcomputer with an LCD panel and overhead projector or even an Internet-connected dumb terminal with a projector are adequate for introductory orientation to the Internet. To train endusers or library staff to use the Internet a lab with Internet-connected computers is essential. Ideally each student should have a computer, but a maximum of two to three people per computer is sometimes the best you can do. The hardware and software choice in the computer lab really should be based on what your library (or university, school, or company) will make available in public areas. For example, if your library makes Macintoshes with Netscape or Mosaic available for public use, then that should be the platform you use for training. If you want to teach e-mail and your site gives all endusers a Unix account with access to the Pine mailer, then you should plan to get the trainees connected to their Unix accounts and using the Pine mailer.

We prefer a mixed laboratory in terms of hardware—that is, some Macintoshes and some Windows machines so that participants can choose the platform with which they feel most comfortable. Each workstation should have a good Web client (such as Netscape or Mosaic) and at least a basic set of helper software (for example, telnet, SoundMachine, etc.). However, even if you just have basic e-mail, telnet, or World Wide Web client access to the Internet, you can offer or participate in Internet training over the Internet— Case 1 describes such a program. Participants can either do "homework" assignments through e-mail or Web pages or interact in real-time through a telnet connection to a text-based virtual reality, such as MUD, MOO, MUCK, or MUSH (see Case 1 for definitions). Soon, it will be possible to interact in real-time through a Web page interface.

WHAT LEVEL AND KIND OF INTERNET TRAINING WILL YOU PROVIDE?

The facilities you have available will be the first factor in deciding whether you will offer hands-on or demonstration-only training. For endusers you might want to offer a sequence of workshops starting with "What is the Internet?" and eventually getting to "How to build your own World Wide Web page." For staff training it is advisable to evaluate what the staff will be using the Internet for. In planning the training described in Case 2 the biggest obstacle to implementing the training was convincing supervisors that staff would be learning something that they would use on the job. Cataloging and interlibrary loan staff will want to learn how to connect to other libraries' catalogs; the reference staff need to learn to identify and evaluate information resources. Sometimes you will need a simple "hook"—like teaching staff e-mail so they can communicate

Case 1   L.O.S.T. (Librarian Online Support Team)
http://www.wlu.edu/~cmorton/lost.html

*Contacts: Isabel Danforth, Librarian, Wethersfield Public Library, Connecticut (danforth@tiac.net)
and Cathy Bennett, Director, Belmont Technical College Library, Ohio (libnm1@nccvax.wvnet.edu)*

The L.O.S.T. (Librarian Online Support Team) project was created to provide training
and mentoring through Diversity University for librarians with limited access to other
training opportunities.

Diversity University is a MOO (MUD object-oriented software). MOOs are one of a
class of software programs, including MUDs (multi-user domains), MUCKs, and
MUSHes, which are interactive environments where many users can connect through
the Internet (or through other kinds of network or through dial-access) and talk to
each other. They can interact with objects and spaces described by text. For the most
part these interactive environments or text-based virtual realities have been used for
gaming; many libraries disallow enduser access to them for that reason. Dozens of
these environments are now being used, however, for scholarly and professional
activities. Diversity University, created by social worker Jeanne McWhorter
(gsswky@menudo.uh.edu), is one of the best of these environments. The idea grew and
is now a complete virtual university where hundreds of teachers and students teach
and learn hundreds of subjects. The objects with which students and teachers interact
are virtual media materials, lecture scripts, computers, blackboards, and even cadavers.
The spaces they move through are classrooms, student centers, and laboratories. There
is even a virtual quadrangle with virtual squirrels! Diversity University, now a nonprofit
corporation, was the site of an Annenberg CPB grant (Susquehanna Univ. was the
actual grant recipient). It is located on a telnet-accessible and World Wide Web-
accessible Unix platform at Stanford University (telnet://moo.du.org:8888 or http://
moo.du.org:8888).

In early 1995, Cathy Bennett and Isabel Danforth were frequent participants in
Diversity University. They were also pursuing their master's degrees in library and
information science. Cathy was studying through an innovative distance education
program from the University of South Carolina that primarily utilized satellite delivery
of content, augmented by e-mail, toll-free telephone access, and intensive in-person
weekend contact.

She also supervised the Learning Center at West Virginia Northern Community
College, New Martinsville regional campus.

Isabel was a student at the Southern Connecticut State University. She and Cathy
were "hanging around talking" in Diversity University one night, discussing the recent
West Virginia State Library System's program, which received federal grant funds to put
its 55 county public libraries on the Internet. West Virginia's county public libraries
would be set up with full graphical Internet POPs (Points of Presence) with 56 kpbs
connections into every county.

The W.V. State Library Commission provided initial setup and training support but
Cathy felt that for many librarians, especially those in the rural, isolated areas of the

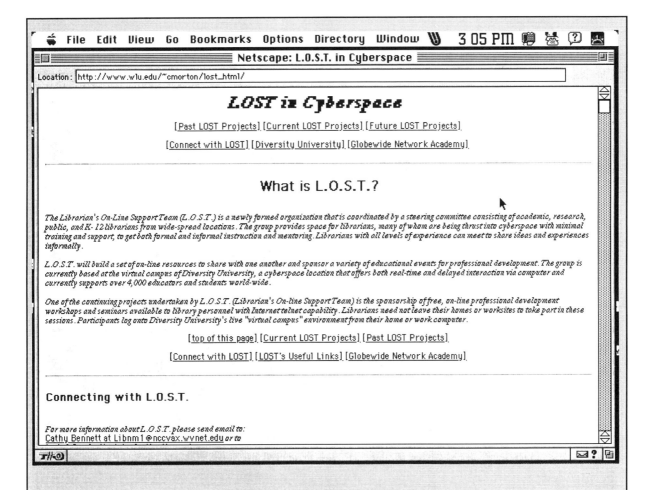

state, some method of ongoing—even daily—support from fellow librarians might be needed and welcomed. Isabel and Cathy recognized that there were many similiarities between West Virginia and Connecticut in the way that librarians were being given net access without intensive support and training. There was often not a local community of librarians in either state to provide mentoring mutual support.

Cathy and Isabel were inspired with the idea of using the facilities of Diversity University as a way to provide Internet training (and mentoring) to West Virginia and Connecticut and to the public librarians in other rural states just getting connected to the Internet. The idea expanded to include Internet mentoring for any librarian, as well as professional development in areas other than Internet.

Cathy and Isabel had only themselves to rely on as staff, and since they both were working and going to school they decided to propose the project as a research project/paper for their degrees. Isabel's instructor at Southern Connecticut State University and Cathy's instructor at the University of South Carolina were both enthusiastic and supportive of the project.

Cathy and Isabel needed no money to fund the project. They began by recruiting volunteer instructors (including one of the authors of this book) whom they trained to deliver lectures in a virtual classroom in Diversity University. They also developed a "steering committee" of professional librarians who volunteered their time to the L.O.S.T. project. Through Diversity University presenters and students can access and demonstrate Internet services like Gopher and World Wide Web. The L.O.S.T. project requires registration from students so that classroom space can be managed. It has offered classes on such Internet topics as identifying and subscribing to discussions lists, computer networking concepts for libraries, copyright, and authoring HTML documents. The L.O.S.T. project has hosted—and will host in the future—discussions with American Library Association President Betty Turock on such important issues as the impact of the Information Superhighway on public libraries.

Both Cathy and Isabel have graduated and both continue to be professional librarians on and off the Internet.

Case 2	Staff Internet Training, Kent State University Libraries, Kent, Ohio

Contacts: Gladys Smiley Bell (gbell@kentvm.kent.edu), Paul Fehrmann (pfehrman@kentvm.kent.edu), Kara Robinson (krobinso@kentvm.kent.edu), Diane K. Kovacs (diane@kovacs.com)

This case is from Diane Kovacs's experience as a reference librarian at Kent State University.

The original idea to provide Internet training to librarians and library staff was mine. Several colleagues (librarians and paraprofessionals) in reference and technical services had asked me to teach them how to use the Internet. Rather than teaching one person at a time I proposed that we develop an Internet training program for all the library staff. Three of my reference colleagues (Gladys Smiley Bell, Paul Fehrmann, and Kara Robinson) were eager to participate in such a project. We took the idea to Barbara Schloman, Head of Information Services, who thought it was a good one. She presented the proposal to the library administration at a meeting of the heads of departments and the Dean of the Libraries. It was harder to sell the idea to library administration than we expected. Our biggest obstacle was the concern on the part of some departmental supervisors that this training was a waste of time or would encourage staff to "play around on the Internet" during working hours.

Our strategy was twofold:

1. Train a group of trainers.
2. Have the trainers group offer training on Internet topics useful to library staff in their professional activities.

It was not difficult to get permission to begin the first part of our training plan. The library already had a small lab with eight DOS computers directly cabled to the Internet, so we planned to do most of the training hands-on. Each trainer picked a topic and worked with me to develop training materials and scripts for that topic. Our team created an Internet training workbook for library staff with each trainer's materials included in the workbook.

The initial training design and creation of training materials took nearly a month. We worked during times we were not scheduled on the reference desk, in meetings, or doing bibliographic instruction—a little more than five hours per week. We practiced our training on each other and then on a group of graduate student employee volunteers.

After we made a point of promising to stress only appropriate uses of the Internet during working hours, our proposal to train the rest of the library staff was approved. Computer services and library systems staff supported our endeavors. For them it meant the prospect of fewer questions.

Our advertising flyer is reproduced in Figure 2.2. It was distributed to library department supervisors, along with a memo requesting them to post it or redistribute it if they felt it would be useful to anyone in their department. We allowed 15 people per session—two per computer; all sessions filled up quickly.

We videotaped the second session of "Using the Internet to Provide Reference Services" and used the video to evaluate our performances. Our evaluations from attendees were uniformly excellent.

Interlibrary loan staff were the first to demonstrate the value of the Internet to traditional library services. They reported that being able to search library catalogs directly sometimes made it much easier to identify and obtain materials for which they had only partial information.

At this writing, the Internet staff training is no longer offered. Internet training for endusers, however, has been developed and implemented by the original trainers group along with graduate students from the Kent State University School of Library and Information Science. This training is offered several times each semester as one-hour or half-hour sessions. Advanced sessions and sessions focusing on specific subjects are also offered. Contact Gladys Smiley Bell for current information.

with their children in college or other relatives around the world—to recruit motivated trainees.

FOR WHOM ARE YOU PROVIDING THE INTERNET TRAINING?

This is an important question that needs to be answered in conjunction with the previous question. Will you be training university, secondary school, or elementary school students? Faculty or teachers? Library staff? The general public? The whole world? You'll need to have a clear idea of your audience. If you will be training the general public it might be a good idea to ask your patrons what they think they want to learn about the Internet. Faculty or teachers would probably like to learn how the Internet can benefit their teaching and researching in their subject specialty. You must be the judge of your training audience. Gather as much information about their needs and wants as you can before designing your training.

DO YOU OR YOUR COLLEAGUES HAVE THE NECESSARY KNOWLEDGE TO PROVIDE GOOD, ACCURATE INTERNET TRAINING AT THE LEVEL YOU'VE CHOSEN?

If you want to teach HTML coding and you need to learn it yourself, there is no shame in looking for an outside trainer. Conversely, if you or other staff have strong knowledge of building Web pages then your only real obstacle is whether you or they have the time to do the training. Judge yourself liberally; we have worked with many people who didn't realize just how much they did know until they started designing the training they wanted to offer.

WHAT INTERNET SERVICES WILL YOU TEACH? WHY?

This might seem like an awfully simple question. In fact, it's an important question that some training developers overlook. You need to ask yourself questions like: Does my training audience have access to full-graphical Web clients like Netscape or only to text clients like Lynx? Will they be likely to want to use FTP to retrieve software and graphics or is that not likely to be something they'd do?

For example, in working with a corporate client to design training for their employees, we found that although they thought they "should" learn FTP they really had no need to. They told us they wanted to use FTP to copy files between employees in different areas of the country, and they wanted to be able to get software. In fact, they had an excellent corporate Intranet across which they could use Eudora to transfer files. They were pleased when they realized that using Eudora instead of FTP meant they could copy formatted files between users. They also had an outstanding Information Systems Department (ISD) which handled all retrieval and installation of software for them—so no enduser would ever need to retrieve or install software. The point is that you should find out what your trainees have access to and why they want to learn different Internet activities. Judge for yourself whether the Internet services you teach are appropriate for your endusers.

What kind of promotion will you have for the training?

How you promote your training may be dictated by how much money or time you want to spend. If you are planning training for the general public, then sending flyers through postal mail or placing ads in newspapers may be good promotional strategies. On the other hand, you might want to put up posters in the library and gauge interest before spending money on mailings or newspaper ads. Figure 2.2 is an example of such a posting for staff training. For more advanced training programs or training for endusers whom you know already have access to a particular system, a notice at the start-up screen on your system or on your Web page or gopher server are good options. These are also great options if you are offering online Internet training. Keep in mind that endusers without access will not see that kind of promotion. Promoting training for people who want to get started by marketing the training online is probably not going to be profitable—posters in your building and other buildings at your site are a much better idea. If you are targeting your training to a particular group, then sending flyers or talking to that group would be an efficient promotion.

Figure 2.2 Library Staff Internet Training Flyer

Internet Training
for
Library Staff

Fall 1993

Attendance Optional
Registration Required:
call x3045 or e-mail to dkovacs@kentvm.kent.edu

1. Basic Introductory Seminar:
    Using the Internet to Provide Reference Services
Date: October 28, 1993 8:00–10:00 a.m.
Limit of 15 participants
Instructors: Gladys Smiley Bell and Diane Kovacs

This is a presentation on the use of Internet resources and tools to answer reference questions. The workshop will address when to use Internet resources at the Reference desk and when to schedule an RBA (Reference by Appointment). It will also address which specific resources are reliable and dependable enough to access and search quickly and which resources are useful when traditional resources fail. Emphasis will be an overview of what other reference librarians are doing and scenarios of possible use. Hands-on exercise will be an actual reference question that participants will answer using Internet resources.
*Participants will receive readings which they will be expected to read before the workshop.

Who Should Attend?
Reference and Information Services staff

2. Electronic Conference Identification and Archives Searching:
    How to Use E-Conferences for Your Own and Patrons' Research
Date: November 16, 1993 8:00–10:00 a.m.
Instructors: Paul Fehrmann and Diane Kovacs

This workshop will cover scholarly E-conferences identification, subscription, and archives searching/back issues retrieval. It will include electronic journals and Gopher archives. Some hands-on exercises are included.

Who Should Attend?
Reference and Information Services staff who require more information on electronic conferences and electronic journals in the context of library services

60-Minute Seminars on Internet-Related Topics

Seminar B	**OhioLINK: The Ohio Library and Information Network**	
Tues.	Sept. 14	10:00a.m.
Wed.	Sept. 29	1:00p.m.

Seminar G	**Internet Navigation Tools**	
Mon.	Sept. 27	noon
Thurs.	Oct. 28	2:00p.m.

Seminar H	**Using Kent's IBM for E-Mail**	
Tues.	Sept. 28	2:00p.m.

Seminar M	**Full-Text Humanities Resources on the Internet**	
Mon.	Oct. 25	10:00a.m.

Workshops Planned for Spring 1994
Internet Basics: FTP and telnet Paul Fehrmann
Electronic Texts and Location Tools: WAIS, ARCHIE
Internet Resource Finding Tools: Gopher/Veronica, Hytelnet and World Wide Web

Please let us know what other workshops you'd be interested in. Send e-mail to dkovacs@kentvm.kent.edu if you have suggestions.

How much time do you estimate it will take to design the training, including the development of training materials?

Every time we've designed training—whether for corporate clients, continuing studies workshops, or staff training—this issue has been a real sticking point. A rule of thumb is to plan on two to three hours of initial preparation time for every one hour you will spend in class. In fact, this will vary with the training you plan to offer. It generally takes a lot longer to plan a good introductory hands-on workshop than a more advanced one. Why? Because you need to try to ensure that the beginners have consistently positive experiences. More advanced learners can cope with occasional failures (due to such things as site outage and hardware/software failure). Once you've designed the training and developed the materials you can just spend a few minutes before every session checking for accuracy and making any changes that seem merited. Of course, you may need to factor in time for you or others to learn what you plan to teach. For example, if you want to include the new HTML tag for frames in the next Web page workshop you teach, you need to make sure you know how to work with frames yourself before you can teach others. Some of the materials we have developed are included in the *Internet Trainer's Guide* (see Appendix E for publication information).

How much time will you have to teach each session, and how will you schedule the sessions?

Many people believe they can teach even an introduction to the Internet in one-half hour or less. The idea is absurd. You might be able to offer a promotional presentation about the Internet but you will not be training anyone about the Internet. If all you have available are half-hour sessions, start with a plan that looks something like the one in Figure 2.3.

Base the length of sessions on the probable availability of your potential audience. College students and faculty generally have 45- to 50-minute blocks available throughout each weekday. The general public may be interested in spending a Saturday afternoon learning about the Internet. A busy teacher may have a half-hour lunch break before she has to pick up her children. Corporate libraries may need to offer training as a series of blocks of time that

Figure 2.3 Outline for a Series of Half-Hour Internet Training Sessions

Session 1
What Is the Internet and Why Should I Use It?

Session 2
Interpersonal E-Mail and Basic Etiquette Using Our Local E-Mail System

Session 3
Identifying and Subscribing to Listserv, Listproc, or Majordomo (managed e-mail discussion groups)

Session 4
Usenet Newsgroups: How to Use the Newsreader Software and Find Good Stuff

Session 5
Identifying Places to Telnet to, and Telneting to Libraries Around the World or Around the Corner

Session 6
Introduction to Netscape, Mosaic, or Lynx: Browsing the Web

Session 7
Introduction to Searching the World Wide Web

Session 8
FTPing Graphics and Software (for those who might want to do that—text files are better accessible through Web)

Session 9
Building Your Own World Wide Web Homepage

Figure 2.4 Example Plan for Corporate Lunchtime Internet Training

Internet Workshop for _____

Daily Schedule of What Will Be Covered

Tuesday, Oct. 17, 11:00 a.m.–1:30 p.m.
11:00–11:30	Introductions and discussion of participants experiences.
11:30–12:30	Overview of course. Focus on issues for business information and marketing on the Internet: security, privacy, marketing, and quality of information.
12:30–1:00	Discussion of basic "netiquette." Finding the right population for marketing and marketing Surveys.
1:00–1:30	E-conferences for business information and marketing.

Wednesday, Oct. 18, 11:00 a.m.–1:30 p.m.
11:00–12:00	Subscribing to e-conferences and e-journals (hands-on). Look at Usenet newsgroups.
12:00–12:30	FTP using Netscape and Anarchie.
12:30–1:00	Archie (demonstration).
1:00–1:30	File transfer issues for Macintosh.

Thursday, Oct. 19, 11:00 a.m.–1:30 p.m.
11:00–12:00	The World Wide Web and marketing.
12:00–12:30	World Wide Web through Netscape.
12:30–1:30	Using Web search tools (Webcrawler).

Friday, Oct. 20, 11:00 a.m.–1:30 p.m.
11:00–1:30	Researching on the Internet. Evaluating business information. Key sites.

---

are not so long that they take people away from their jobs for an entire day but that aren't so short that the trip into the headquarters office isn't worthwhile. Long lunch-time sessions also can be a possibility. Figures 2.4 and 2.5 offer two possible agendas.

HOW MANY PEOPLE WILL BE NEEDED TO PROVIDE THE TRAINING?

The answer to this question will depend on how many sessions you want to offer and whether you will offer hands-on training. Some libraries have a designated training librarian who may or may not work with other librarians to offer training. Most libraries have to

Figure 2.5   Example Plan for Corporate Internet Training in Two Half-Day Sessions

Session 1	**Business Research on the Internet: Getting Started with the Basics**
1:00–1:30	Introduction to internet addressing and URLs (history and background on handouts only).
1:30–2:30	Exercise 1. Netscape overview: focus on using URLs and setting bookmarks (working from the custom homepage created for the company by the trainer).
2:30–2:45	Discussion of basic "netiquette": emoticons, acronyms, flaming, rtfm, etc.
2:45–3:00	Break
3:00–4:00	Exercise 2. Using Internet e-mail for business communications. (After a tour of the mailer, participants will send e-mail to the trainer's e-mail address, to the president, or to any address of their choice.)
4:00–4:30	Exercise 3. Identifying and subscribing to e-conferences (discussion lists, listservs, etc.)
4:30–5:00	Exercise 4. Telnet and Hytelnet (through Netscape).

Session 2	**Business Research on the Internet: Getting to Work**
1:00–1:15	Critical issues for business users of the Internet: privacy, security, accuracy, and timeliness.
1:15–2:15	Exercise 1. Overview of Netscape (review).
2:15–2:45	Exercise 2. Gopher and Veronica (through Netscape).
2:45–3:00	Break
3:00–4:00	Exercise 3. Using Web search tools (Infoseek, Excite, Webcrawler, Yahoo, Lycos, etc.).
4:00–4:30	Exercise 4. Researching on the Internet. Participants have the choice of using a prepared business research question list provided by the instructor, or writing 3 to 5 of their own questions and researching and reporting them.
4:30–5:00	Exercise 5. Key sites on the Internet for your company (working from the custom homepage created for the company by the trainer).

rely on librarians to do training in addition to their regular duties. In the former instance, the training librarian can best decide how many sessions he or she can offer. In the latter, the entire schedule of activities in which librarians participate must be considered.

Hands-on training can be very difficult for one person to manage. A professional trainer can generally handle approximately 20 hands-on trainees—with any more than 20 a co-trainer is highly desirable. Most librarians are not professional trainers, so if you are offering hands-on training a co-trainer will make the training much more enjoyable and profitable for both the trainers and the participants.

We recommend a team approach to offering training. Establish a group of librarians who can focus on the training they need to become good Internet trainers, let them train and practice with each other, and then distribute the burden of training among the team members.

In online training it can help to have someone standing by to assist with answering questions. Text-based, virtual interactive sessions are very much like hands-on sessions: it is also helpful to have more than one trainer online with you to assist participants in such sessions.

WHAT MECHANISMS WILL YOU USE TO EVALUATE THE EFFECTIVENESS OF THE TRAINING?

Most trainers use evaluation forms or questionnaires that participants complete. These are helpful for discovering if participants' needs have been met. Even if you're teaching remotely you can collect e-mailed or Web page evaluation forms. Such forms are not necessarily useful, however, for evaluating the quality of the training itself—evaluations can reflect biases such as whether the participants liked the trainers, were in a bad mood that day, or simply were not prepared for a specific level of training. Once when we taught a one-day hands-on introduction to using the Internet for research, one of the participants wrote on her evaluation form that "There was too much messing around with computers."

Videotaping training sessions is an excellent way to evaluate the quality of training. It gives the trainers a clear idea of their presentation style and they can watch the faces and actions of participants at their leisure. Peer reviewing, where an observer—preferably another member of the Internet training team—participates in the training, with the primary goal of evaluating the trainer, is similarly helpful.

IMPLEMENTATION

Implementation begins with the planning phase. Once the trainer or trainers have completed planning, they are now ready to design and create materials, and schedule and market the sessions. In our experience it makes sense first to design and create the materials and then to schedule the sessions. The reason for this is that the preparation of the session may give you a much better idea of how long the training session will take. Also if you have the materials ready, when you begin to promote the sessions you can provide interested participants with a very clear idea of what will be covered—what prerequisites will be necessary.

MAINTENANCE

Once the training is planned, designed, scheduled, and presented, you'll want to collect the evaluations—in whatever form—and assess the training. Then it's time to decide on revisions in the training design or even if you want to teach a given session again. Periodically repeat the process of designing, materials preparation, scheduling, and marketing. It helps to have good clerical support; a skilled clerk or secretary can often take over much of the materials revisions and preparation after the initial design and preparation.

SUMMARY

Internet training can be the key to creating an image of the library as a valuable resource for your endusers. The library will also be identified in endusers' minds as the place to turn for research assistance when they are using the Internet. Offering Internet training defines the future of librarians as information brokers.

Chapter 3

Offering and Marketing Traditional Library Services Through the Internet

Offering library services through the Internet serves many excellent purposes: it enhances access to library services, it promotes library services, and it creates a good feeling for the library.

In this chapter the case descriptions are real-life examples written by librarians who use the Internet to market their library's services. We discovered that many public, university, and special libraries use interpersonal e-mail, Gopher, and the World Wide Web to offer and market traditional library services. These libraries see the offering of traditional library services through the Internet as a mechanism for promoting those library services and enhancing a positive image of the library among their community of endusers.

The key issues to consider when planning to offer or market library services through the Internet are: To whom are you offering or marketing library services? and What library services do you offer that you would want to offer or market through the Internet? Figure 3.1 outlines questions specific to planning for library marketing on the Internet. These questions are discussed below.

Figure 3.1 Questions to Ask in Planning to Offer or Market Traditional Library Services Through the Internet

1. To whom are you providing library services? To whom would you like to be providing library services?

2. What kind of Internet connectivity is available to your community of endusers?

3. What kind of library services will you offer?

4. Do you or others in your organization have the skills and knowledge to create a Web page or Gopher, or to manage an e-mail reference or information service?

5. What Internet service(s) will you use? Why?

6. How much time do you estimate it will take to plan, implement, and maintain the project?

7. How many people will be needed to plan, implement, and maintain the project?

PLANNING

TO WHOM ARE YOU PROVIDING LIBRARY SERVICES? TO WHOM WOULD YOU LIKE TO BE PROVIDING LIBRARY SERVICES?

All libraries have a core user group. Internet access to library services can enhance service to the core group of endusers. All of the case descriptions in this chapter touch on that aspect. You can also use Internet access for the following purposes:

Provide new services for your core user group. Diana Jarvis and Karl Pearson (see Case 3) and Rita Reisman (see Case 4) describe the ways in which, through e-mail, the Lockheed Martin Technical Operations Library and the ITT Aerospace/Communications Division Library have "boosted library use" and created more positive attitudes about the library. Both libraries offer personal customer

Case 3	Lockheed Martin Technical Operations Library, Sunnyvale, California

Contact: Diana Jarvis and Karl Pearson (pills@svpal.org)

Our little library is tucked away in a small space off-site from the users we serve, and it has a miniscule circulating collection. We weren't able to offer much until the Air Force customer we support installed an extensive LAN with e-mail. This gave us an excellent channel for promoting our services by e-mailing to everyone on a weekly basis a short newsletter or book review, for taking reference requests, and for delivering answers with no delay. Then we got onto the Internet and vastly expanded the resources we can draw upon. Now we've boosted usage of the library to more than 350 active users by serving as their "personal information agent" and delivering "at-your-desk" information services. Thanks to an inter-building delivery service, we can provide hard-copy materials without users having to stir from their own offices.

Case 4	ITT Aerospace/Communications Division Library, Clifton, New Jersey

Contact: Rita Reisman (reisman@vaxa.acdnj.itt.com)

I have established profiles of information various engineers have requested (with CARL UNCOVER), and I send it electronically to each individual as the topics come in. The service is good, because it covers a much wider serial base than we could ever hope to acquire—especially with downsizing and budget cuts. I've received some positive feedback on it even though the service is still in the early stages.

service and personalized information delivery through e-mail to their endusers.

Attract new endusers. Most of the cases describe the library as attracting new users through its Internet services. Sarah Mack (see Case 5) describes the impact of the West Bloomfield Township Public Library's Web page through which the library markets Internet workshops and other library services.

Better serve endusers who are underserved. Underserved endusers are the folks who either don't have time or don't like to come to the library. Jian Liu (see Case 6) discusses the expansion of the Indiana University Libraries' "Ask a Librarian" service.

Case 5   West Bloomfield Township Public Library, West Bloomfield, Michigan

Contact: Sarah Mack (macksara@metronet.lib.mi.us)

Our library is using our homepage (http://metronet.lib.mi.us/WEST/wbpl.html) to reach out to the local community on a variety of levels. This service is fairly new. I've been working on it since early summer 1995 and I uploaded it to our server in December 1995. By the end of January we will have added a section on the community. In addition to designing the Web site, I have been teaching Internet workshops at the library since January 1995; that has proved a tremendous marketing tool for us. People who have lived here for 20 years and never visited are coming in for the class, finding out about our services, and getting library cards.

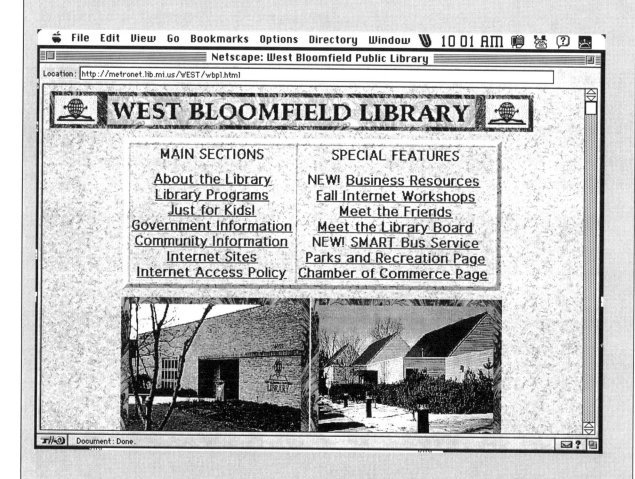

Case 6   Indiana University Libraries, Bloomington, Indiana
http://www.indiana.edu/~libweb/question.html

Contact: Jian Liu (jiliu@indiana.edu)

During the pre-Web days, we offered reference services via e-mail on the campus VMS system in a closed environment. That service was quite successful, especially among faculty members. Then began the long and confusing process of migrating off the VMS to the Web environment, during which many of our regular customers lost us.

Among the first things the Research Collections and Services Department did when our Web page was brought up was to offer reference service through the Web. Again, we called it "Ask a Librarian." It is available on our homepage at http://www.indiana.edu/~librcsd/ as well as on most of the linked pages on our server. Later, the option is extended to the Web server for the entire library.

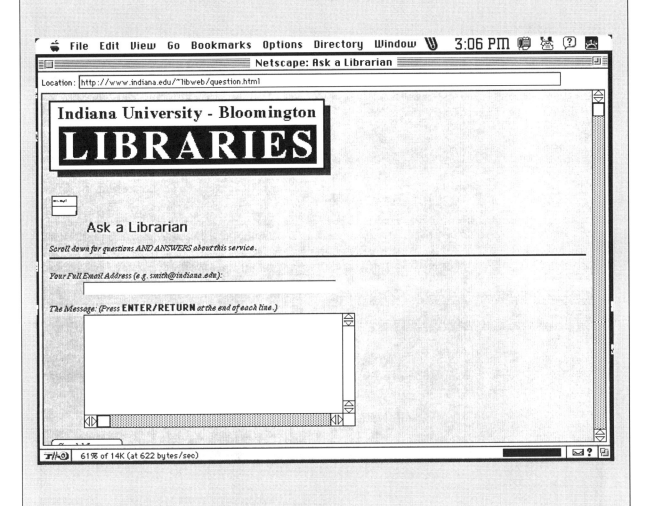

My colleagues in the Reference Department monitor the incoming questions frequently, and always try to get back to the patrons as soon as possible. In our replies to patron questions, we include our direct e-mail address, our phone number, and the URL for our Web page. We use every opportunity to assure our patrons that we are available to help them.

Our efforts are beginning to pay back. We are seeing a steady increase in the use of the service. We have gradually regained our old customers and we have "seen" more and more new users. I'd say our "Ask a Librarian" service is fairly established among the university community.

What kind of Internet connectivity is available to your community of endusers?

This question is critical. Your intended endusers must have access to the kind of Internet service through which you will offer your library services. It's not sensible to offer highly graphical Web services to endusers who don't have access to graphical Web clients. You may have to focus on text-based services even when offering your service through a Web page.

Large university and college libraries can usually depend on the majority of their endusers having at least laboratory access to graphical Web clients such as Netscape or Mosaic. They can also find out if their school makes computer accounts available to at least some of their endusers. These accounts should have some kind of Web access, such as Lynx.

Some libraries offer Internet computer accounts to their endusers. Michael Schuyler (see Case 7) describes the Kitsap Regional Library's more than 10,000 registered users. Kitsap provides endusers with e-mail, Gopher, and Web access.

It's also reasonable to provide an on-site laboratory with access to graphical Web clients. Still others provide multiple access possibilities. Chapter 4 describes the Cleveland Public Library's electronic library. It can be reached through a graphical Web client, or users can dial up directly and use Lynx to browse it. Lourdes Mordini (see Case 8) describes a similar accomodation at the North Suburban Library System.

Case 7   Kitsap Regional Library, Washington

Contact: Michael Schuyler (michael@linknet.kitsap.lib.wa.us)

Kitsap Regional Library is offering Internet access as well as traditional library services; you're welcome to come over and take a look. We have a Web page up at linknet.kitsap.lib.wa.us as well as a Gopher. We have 10,000 registered users of our system, where we also provide e-mail. If you want a registered user account to see how it looks, just telnet to the above address, sign on as a guest, and fill out the new user registration form.

Case 8   North Suburban Library System, Illinois
http://listserv.nsls.lus.org

Contact: Lourdes Mordini (lmordini@nslsilus.org)

The North Suburban Library System covers all types of libraries located in the suburbs north of Chicago. Several months ago we started a project of disseminating local and regional information through NorthStarNet (NSN), a network of Web pages provided by the local public libraries and links to useful patron-oriented information. Some of us are including such items as our quarterly newsletters, schedules, bibliographies, and bookmobile schedules. This could be seen as a form of library promotion. It is a great public service. Our patrons can access NSN with a telephone and modem; they do not need to have an Internet account. Of course NSN can also be reached through the Internet.

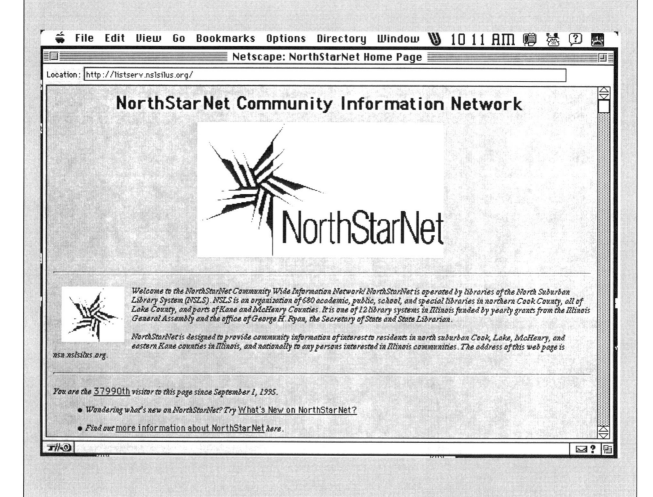

WHAT KIND OF LIBRARY SERVICES WILL YOU OFFER?

What kind of library services do you offer on-site and in-person? Most of these can be adapted for Internet access. Scott Anderson (see Case 9) presents an excellent example of almost every possible library service being offered by the Ganser Library at Millersville University through their Web page. Services include:

- schedules and policies, and documentation of library services
- announcements of training and other library events
- resource guides and bibliographies
- interlibrary loan requests and new book recommendations
- reference services
- special databases created locally

Access to locally created databases is also described in Case 10 and is addressed again in Chapter 6.

Four other innovative applications introduced in academic libraries are presented in Cases 11–14.

DO YOU OR OTHERS IN YOUR ORGANIZATION HAVE THE SKILLS AND KNOWLEDGE TO CREATE A WEB PAGE OR GOPHER, OR TO MANAGE AN E-MAIL REFERENCE OR INFORMATION SERVICE?

All you'll really need to know—in addition to being competent to provide good library service—is basic e-mail for your local system and, possibly, how to use HTML to create Web pages. You may need computer systems people to run some Web servers for you or programmers to write CGI or Java scripts for you. Actually, you can find many ready-made scripts for such things as counting, gathering survey information, and tabulating forms answers—although you'll need a Webmaster who can install and run them.

WHAT INTERNET SERVICE(S) WILL YOU USE? WHY?

All of the case descriptions in this chapter discuss using either e-mail or the World Wide Web, or a combination of the two. As discussed in Chapter 1, you may also want to use Gopher if that's what you have access to. Otherwise, e-mail and the Web are currently the best ways to provide and/or market library services through the Internet.

**Case 9   Ganser Library, Millersville University, Millersville, Pennsylvania
http://www.millersv.edu/~library/index.html**

Contact: Scott Anderson (sanderso@marauder.millersv.edu)

We're still under construction so if you visit, wear your hard hat.
   Basically, as the library's "Webmaster," I'm trying to do just a few simple things:

- **Static Documentation.** This is the stuff that usually gets issued as an important memo or nifty little packet (primarily circulation policies), but you can never find when you need it, and if you do manage to find it, is it the latest version?
- **Interlibrary Loan Requests.** Currently I'm beholden to a much understaffed and overworked computing department on campus for the programming that makes forms possible, so I'm in the learning curve for bringing that process "in-house." Eventually the director would like the library to dispense with filling out paper forms for requesting materials and to handle the process electronically.
- **Ordering Materials.** Similar to the forms for ILL requests, ordering new materials will most likely be handled electronically as well.

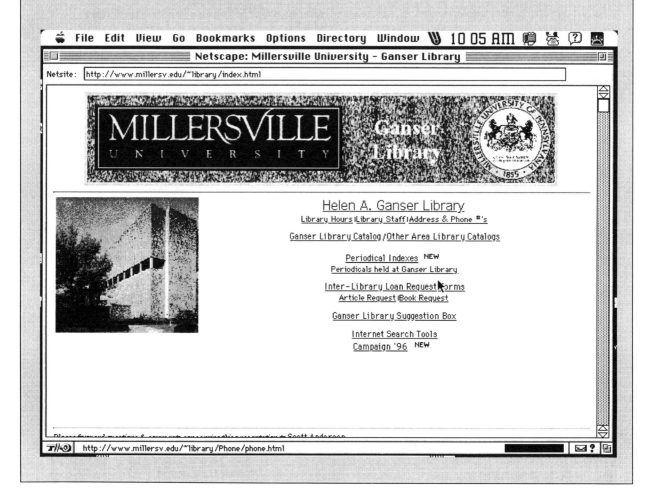

- **What's New!** Many libraries publish that "recent acquisitions" list and then send it off to faculty across campus. I'd like to see part of that done here at Millersville, except electronically.
- **Resource Guides.** I can't stand the library copy machine, so several of the librarians have started to post "bibliographies" for particular classes on the library's homepage instead of trying to track down the librarian that generated it when a student comes to reference with the "I lost the handout" story. This idea fits into a larger instructional and information literacy program within the library.

Some type of self-guided tour of the library is also lurking around in the back of my mind, when I get the time, steal the time, manufacture the time. . . .
We're at http://www.millersv.edu/~library/HP.html if you'd like to take a look.

HOW MUCH TIME DO YOU ESTIMATE IT WILL TAKE TO PLAN, IMPLEMENT, AND MAINTAIN THE PROJECT?

The amount of time you put in will depend on what you want to do. Some of the case descriptions in this chapter could qualify as the kind of electronic libraries described in Chapter 4. Obviously, that level of service will require more time than a simple Web page with a few policies and schedules, announcements, and library guides.

HOW MANY PEOPLE WILL BE NEEDED TO PLAN, IMPLEMENT, AND MAINTAIN THE PROJECT?

Most of us use committees for planning library projects. How many people make up the project planning committee and their role will depend on your local policies. After the planning is finished, one or two people can implement and maintain most projects. For interlibrary loan or book ordering, the people receiving the requests (usually via e-mailed forms) will probably be the same people who are now in charge of regular ILL and book ordering. The same will apply for reference services. In fact, reference service through the Internet can be managed similarly to in-person or phone reference, by scheduling reference staff for duty at different times. After a few months, the Internet services will become part of the library staff's regular routine.

Case 10   Queensland University of Technology Library, Brisbane, Australia

Contact: Barbara Ewers (b.ewers@qut.edu.au)

I have recently put up a Web page (http://www.qut.edu.au/library/irel.html) to publicise IREL, the Australian Industrial Relations Database produced by QUT Library. The page mainly publicises the existence of IREL, its coverage and content, access via OZLINE and Informit, and the commercial searches and document delivery we will undertake for nonstaff and students. I have just started work on the page and hope to exploit its advantages more in the future. I would be interested in joining a group to discuss issues this involves.

I am also leading a team of QUT Library staff which is working on better promoting our services to university clients. We see the Library homepage (http://qut.edu.au/library/) as an important part of this.

File   Edit   View   Go   Bookmarks   Options   Directory   Window   10 00 AM

Netscape: IREL, QUT Library

Location: http://www.qut.edu.au/library/irel.html

[The Library, Queensland University of Technology.]

QUT

IREL
Australian Industrial Relations Database

IREL is the Australian Industrial Relations Database produced by the Queensland University of Technology. The database includes literature on workplace reform and the relationship between unions, employer groups, governments and industrial tribunals. The perspectives of both management and the workforce are represented. Issues such as industrial conflict, wages and conditions, the labour market, equal employment opportunities, occupational health and safety are all well represented in IREL. Records include citations, abstracts, descriptors and identifiers and provide access to industrial relations information not readily available elsewhere.

- Coverage
- Access
- Document Supply

- Subject Scope
- User Guide
- More Information

COVERAGE

The material is exclusively Australian and includes monographs, academic and current affairs journals, as well as more specialised publications such as trade union and employer groups' news letters, working papers and reports, parliamentary papers and conference proceedings.

Newspapers, legal sources of information and awards are not included. A list of the journals indexed is available.

Indexing of IREL began in 1983. The database is updated monthly with approximately 100 records being added each month. In July 1995, IREL contained 14,000 records.

Document : Done.

CASE STUDIES IMPLEMENTATION

If you've followed a strategy similar to the one recommended above, implementation will be fairly simple.

You are ready to create your Web page based on your plans. The most important part of implementation is announcing the availability of your Web page or e-mail service. E-mail distribution or news announcements on your library's system will suffice for your core users and endusers who have Internet access. If financially feasible, it's a good idea to announce your new access in local or campus newspapers. Some libraries might even have access to cable television programs or local news networks; some of our local television stations look for this kind of positive story.

MAINTENANCE

Maintenance of library services on the Internet requires continuous updating of any information provided, and continuous training and availability of personnel to respond to reference and other questions. Clerical and administrative staff should be trained and made responsible for keeping information updated on Web pages.

SUMMARY

Offering library services through the Internet is natural. It is our job to meet our endusers' information needs as much as possible, and our endusers are clearly finding the Internet to be an important source of information. Libraries must be ready to meet those users on the Internet.

Case 11　Iowa State University Libraries, Ames, Iowa
http://www.public.iastate.edu/~cyberstacks/

Contact: Gerry McKiernan (gerrymck@iastate.edu)

I recently announced a new demonstration prototype service called CyberStacks(sm). Over the coming months, I will be enlarging this resource to include a select group of discrete, significant WWW and other Internet science and technology reference resources.

To support development of the service I will be involved with what I believe to be an innovative funding initiative. Once CyberStacks(sm) has sufficient resources, I plan to announce it. Presently I am mulling over a marketing strategy and am quite excited by the possibilities!

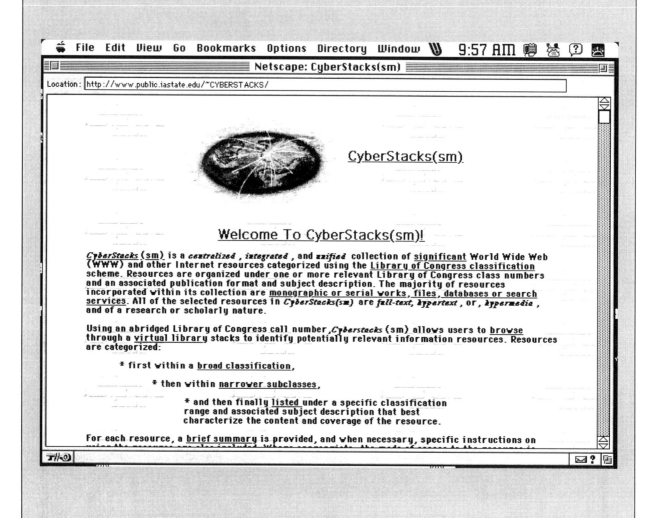

Case 12   University of Southern Queensland Libraries, Queensland, Australia http://www.usq.edu.au/library/index.htm

Contact: Stephen Purcell (purcell@po.usq.edu.au)

Here at the University of Southern Queensland, the library actively engages in public relations. We publish our *USQ News* every two weeks and the *Library Lines* newsletter. The library makes the USQ community aware of the Internet and its resources through demonstrations, training classes, flyers, and speaking engagements. The library has a marketing team, which along with traditional marketing methods also uses the library homepage to market library events.

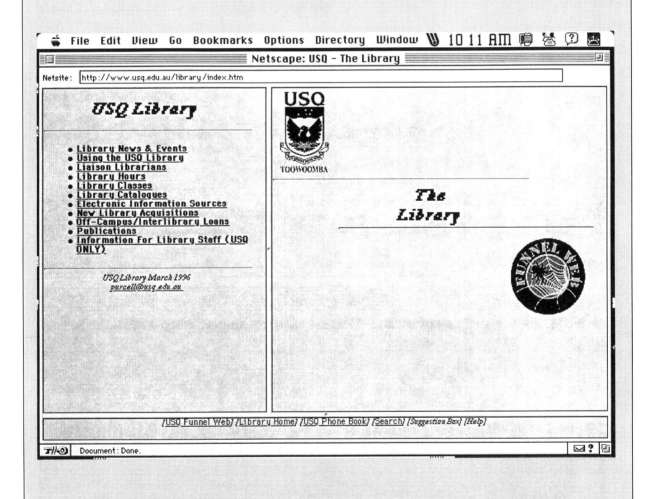

Case 13   Zimmerman Library, University of New Mexico, Albuquerque, New Mexico

Contact: Linda St. Clair (lstclair@unm.edu)

The University of New Mexico General Library is currently developing its Web page. Library News can be seen at http://www.unm.edu/~libinfo/newlibraries.html.

Under Workshops and Tutoring we provide information about library instruction sessions, including the schedule for instruction sessions, relevant instruction policies, and an electronic instruction request form.

Other services offered include electronic reference, interlibrary loan, and call-ins.

We continue to examine other possibilities for developing new methods of marketing library services.

Case 14   Busse Center Library, Mount Mercy College, Cedar Rapids, Iowa

Contact: Linda Scarth (lscarth@mmc.mtmercy.edu)

The Busse Center Library serves a student body of 1,200 in a small city with several other colleges and two universities within easy commuting distance. As an Iowa Open Access library, we are used by the public and by students from the nearby institutions. The campus computer center is part of the library.

The integration of digital and so-called traditional resources is implicit in how we are organized and work. Information content takes precedence over format. The physical and the virtual exist side by side. Much of what we do can be seen as performing traditional library services with newer means of access. The Busse Library Information System (BLIS) PACs offer Windows-based access to our catalog, electronic periodical indexes, other databases, WinGopher, and Netscape. Students with accounts use the Sun workstations in the computer center for e-mail and personal recreational Netscape forays.

The college has a homepage to which the Library Resources page (http://www.mtmercy.edu/busse.html) is linked. The Mount Mercy College homepage (http://www.mtmercy.edu) is the current default Netscape page on the PACs. We plan to change the default on the PACs to the Busse Center Library homepage. We currently have the college page to introduce students, faculty, and the administration to the idea of the World Wide Web and our access and contributions.

Included here are several examples of how we use the Internet to enhance our collection, serve our users, and market our resources and services. The premise underlying the access and arrangement we offer is that the library and the college are the source and that the actual location of information is of minor importance. Because of emphasis on information, we do not include many graphics on our pages. We may add a bit more later.

Information about the library includes hypertext links to some of our guides and learning aids. Some exist in both paper and electronic format as HTML files. The telnet link to Horizon (our catalog) for off-site users is on a menu of other types of links. At this writing, the links Beyond the Horizon include Desktop Library, Curriculum Resources on the Web, Other Libraries, Journals on the Web, Job Search on the Web, Search the World Wide Web, and Ask the Librarian. The Desktop Library is a set of links to far-flung ready-reference type materials.

The Curriculum Resources on the Web page is arranged around the seven academic divisions in the college. Basic useful links for the disciplines within a division are included. I ask faculty about types of Internet resources that they want students to use and I then link appropriate sites. Faculty and students are encouraged to suggest URLs. We find that novices like having this type of introduction to using the WWW. The information is out there in cyberspace, but they found it in the library or through the library homepage.

The Journals on the Web page includes the homepages of some of the periodicals to which we subscribe. Plans are for it to include links to some discipline-related periodicals to which we do not subscribe. Another spinoff will be a set of links to newspapers on the Web. We will promote the library by inviting the campus community to suggest newspapers for these links; that may encourage some users to browse the WWW. One of our exchange students reads the online version of a European newspaper regularly. A reporter for the college newspaper plans a feature article on the library homepage and we will use her article to invite suggestions. The journals and newspaper pages will have links to my page on how to cite the World Wide Web.

The Job Search on the Web page is an example of how we try to connect resources in the library with those found elsewhere. In addition to links to job databanks, it also has a link to a bibliography of resume writing books held by the library. When the campus career office has its own page, these will also appear there.

To make users aware of various ways to search the WWW, and to offer a back door into keyword searching of the Web, we have the Search the World Wide Web choice which links to several major search engines. There is a brief explanation of using menus, search engines, and known URLs to find information.

The Ask the Librarian link is provided to capitalize on student/staff/faculty curiosity and to provide an e-mail reference service. I think it will be more heavily used once the campus is networked and as more users access the library from home. Faculty already make requests by e-mail without the prompt of the homepage. I see this as expanding access and marketing.

Two of the more interesting messages that I have received were from persons who found us while Web surfing. One was a request from someone employed in a company that I believe has all but eliminated its library. He wanted to know if we provided online services commercially. Although we do not offer such service, we do occasional searches for business persons in the area. I invited him to use the library and told him of some of our resources that may be useful to him. It is part of our public relations effort.

The other message came from an alum who happened on our Web page and wanted to know about activities of the alumni office. This we will use in two ways: to promote the library and college to this person in another state and to encourage the college alumni office to let the library help them develop their own page.

We have also added links to several URLs (for example, U.S. Census) in our catalog, again to demonstrate the integration of resources and emphasize the local access point.

On campus we use our Internet access to foster the creativity of students. When graphics design students are learning to design Web pages, we assist them in viewing their progress on the reference PACs. I teach classes in many disciplines about all our resources and how to use, evaluate, and enjoy the intellectual challenges they offer. Remote and local resources are included. I sometimes teach students from other colleges how to use the PACs at their institutions using WinGopher or Netscape. In addition to viewing the resources beyond our walls, we also use the Internet for interlibrary loan with the ARIEL software.

There is nothing exotic about the services offered or used. The Internet can be used by a small academic library to provide service, to promote itself to its own community and constituency, and to be both a physical and a virtual resource.

Chapter 4

Electronic Libraries

An electronic library is probably the most complex information product that you might choose. Prior to World Wide Web and Gopher servers, an electronic library was impractical for the average library to create. Not only did it require complex programming, but it also required some mechanism to make it available to users through telephone dial-up or a network. Cleveland Public Library (Case 11) initially had such a dial-up arrangement and considered some other kinds of networks before deciding on the Internet as the access mechanism for its electronic library.

A World Wide Web server is usually the best tool because it lets you incorporate graphics, sounds, and video. But those who serve endusers without graphics or sound capability will find that text-only access to Web pages is an efficient distribution option. Gopher servers used to be the choice for text-based information, but they are rapidly becoming obsolete or taking on Web server-like functionality.

School libraries might find that the World Wide Web presents problems—like pictures of naked humans. A Gopher or Lynx-only access to a Web server are perhaps safer choices in communities where parents might object to even the potential for accessing such pictures. Text-only access would not solve the problem, but it has been used frequently as a temporary measure until the school establishes workable policies with its community.

In planning for an electronic library on the Internet it helps to consider the questions such as those outlined in Figure 4.1.

Case 15 *The Cleveland Public Libraries' Electronic Library*
http://www.cpl.org

Contact: Bob Carterette, Automation Systems Manager, Cleveland Public Library
(bob@library.cpl.org)

The Cleveland Public Libraries' electronic library (CPEL) project is an outstanding example of a general electronic library. The CPEL began as a collaboration between Bob Carterette, Automation Systems Manager and the Director of Cleveland Public Library. The project was implemented by the Automation Services Department as a part of their regular duties. Although the two principals did not write a project plan or proposal they had a clear idea of what they wanted to do. Their original intention was to model library services for remote users on the traditional organization. Part of their motivation in creating the CPEL was also to preserve the role of the public library in the electronic environment. The CPEL's core goal was to provide organized remote access to networked information resources. The Cleveland Public Library is the core system of a regional library consortium called CLEVNET. The intention is for all users at all CLEVNET sites to have similar library experiences whether they are at the main branch or in Brunswick, Ohio.

The CPEL went online in 1989 running on a VAX cluster, using a proprietary DECnet network. The choice of platform was related to their automation with the Data Research Association (DRA) integrated Library system in 1979. In 1990, they registered an Internet domain name and began migrating the project over to Internet access. They considered using a closed X.25 network to enhance security when they first began offering FirstSearch Databases in 1992. But "We were then totally committed to exploring the Internet as a transport for information services." They chose to use the freely available gopher server software for VAX/VMS to create CPEL. Local enhancements of the software were made by their programming staff. They also implemented dial-in access to their catalog and databases at around the same time.

The CPEL opened to the public through the Internet in August 1993. Since they had used their existing computer platform and free software, the only costs were in significant time spent by three or four Automation Department staff to design and build the CPEL, learn the gopher server installation and program the enhancements and the $20–25,000 for their Internet connection.

In January, 1996, the CPEL has been migrated to the World Wide Web. Dial-access users connect to a Lynx based browser. The Cleveland Public Library now also offers SLIP and PPP public access dial-up to the CPEL. The Web site is a product of a collaboration between the Automation Services, Publicity, Graphics, and Planning and Research Departments of the library.

Figure 4.1   Questions to Ask in Planning an Internet Electronic Library

1. Does your site already have an appropriate level of Internet connectivity to run a Gopher or World Wide Web server?

2. For whom are you providing the electronic library? What kind of Internet connectivity is available to them?

3. To what Internet and other electronic resources will you link through your electronic library? How will you organize them? By subject? By resource type? By type of library service?

4. Do you have personnel who are knowledgeable enough to produce and maintain an electronic library by managing a Gopher or World Wide Web server?

5. Will you use Gopher or the World Wide Web?

6. What computer hardware and software is already available to you through your library, company, or organization?

7. What computer hardware and software will you need to purchase or otherwise acquire?

8. How much time do you estimate it will take to plan, implement, and maintain the electronic library?

9. How many people will be needed to plan, implement, and maintain the service?

PLANNING

DOES YOUR SITE ALREADY HAVE AN APPROPRIATE LEVEL OF INTERNET CONNECTIVITY TO RUN A GOPHER OR WORLD WIDE WEB SERVER?

This is critical. You will need a minimum Internet access of either a two-way ISDN connection or a 56 kbps dedicated Internet connection. In Chapter 1 we discussed some options for platforms. In the appendixes you'll find a list of sources on the Internet for server software.

FOR WHOM ARE YOU PROVIDING THE ELECTRONIC LIBRARY? WHAT KIND OF INTERNET CONNECTIVITY IS AVAILABLE TO THEM?

As discussed in Chapter 3, all libraries have a core user group. An Internet-accessible electronic library will

- enhance service to the core group of endusers
- provide new services for your core user group
- attract new endusers
- better serve endusers who are underserved

It is up to you to decide who you want to serve. Purdue University Libraries (Case 16) defined the target groups for their electronic government documents library. Their proposal is reproduced as Figure 4.2.

TO WHAT INTERNET AND OTHER ELECTRONIC RESOURCES WILL YOU LINK THROUGH YOUR ELECTRONIC LIBRARY? HOW WILL YOU ORGANIZE THEM? BY SUBJECT? BY RESOURCE TYPE? BY TYPE OF LIBRARY SERVICE?

Both of the electronic libraries described in this chapter started with a collection development plan. Cleveland Public Library's intention was to model library services for remote users on the traditional organization; in other words, they intended to move significant services of the library into cyberspace.

The key service that Cleveland Public Library makes available

Figure 4.2   Purdue University Libraries' Proposal for the "GPO Access on the Web" Project

The GPO makes several databases available on-line, including the *Federal Register*, the *Congressional Record* and others. Until recently the depository libraries were limited to one free workstation per library. Now the Government Printing Office (GPO) is now permitting depository libraries to operate servers with up to 10 work stations connected to the GPO's computer. Now it appears that the GPO is interested in providing a World Wide Web front end to *the Federal Register, Congressional Record* and current Bills in Congress.

The GPO uses commercial WAIS to index and disseminate its products. With the current implementation of the software, fielded searching is not possible, but it appears possible to provide Boolean searching using, AND, OR and NOT as well as nested searching. By providing a front end on our web server to the GPO's WAIS server, we can provide a state of the art user interface for campus and other users world wide. This is accomplished by installing and debugging one of several products that are freely available on the Internet. Some of the available products are:

- waissearch 2.02 from CNIDR (part of the freeWais 2.20 package)
- WWWWAIS from EIT
- kindofwais.pl from NCSA
- SFgate from Germany (an unlikely candidate)

All of the above products are available on a no charge basis for University use.

Each of the products will let us convert from WWW to WAIS transparently thus saving the end users from learning yet another front end.

The ITD networking group has already installed one gateway and has discovered some of the problems related to this technology. The GPO requirement of limiting depository libraries to 10 simultaneous uses means that we will have to do some additional programming so that we can control number of users. We estimate that is will take approximately 1/2 time employee for four months to install the software and make it operable with the GPO server. Additionally, some testing of the client must be done with users to determine what layout and instructions will work best. The client testing will take 30 to 60 days and require interaction with the screen design committee.

One overall concern that We have is that this could be too much of a good thing. The GPO wants depository Libraries to provide service to a wide range of patrons on and off campus. On the other hand the GPO wants to limit simultaneous access from any depository site to ten users. This should be useful in protecting the Purdue Internet connection when combined with an active promotion to make our work freely available to other organizations on the network. A successful project will bring a great deal of favorable press to the Libraries for work on a unique technology project. The Libraries is not known as a leader in on-line cutting edge technology services. This project could go a long way in turning that perception around.

Other benefits include the savings accrued from subscription cancellation and immediacy of the information. The University has at least 8 subscriptions to the hard copy of the *Federal Register*, which costs approximately $ 4320.00 ($540.00 each). This project might permit the University to drop many of the paid subscriptions to the *Register* while providing advanced keyword searching for all networked users, no matter what type of computer they are using. This convenience will greatly add to the productivity of our researchers that are seeking government grants and for our administrators that need to stay on top of the daily changes to federal law. It is possible to obtain electronic access to the *Federal Register* but the cost is anywhere from $5,000 to $10,000 per year. My understanding is that Gaines "Buddy" Miles in the Department of Sponsored Programs is looking at such a product. By investing a small cost in some student labor and a minimal amount of software the University has campus wide access at a very small cost $1,920 for labor and two copies of SoftQuad's HTML editor at $80.00 per copy.

In Summary this project will take approximately .5 student labor for 4 months to develop, test, and implement the service. Some of the student labor will be used to give release time to the full time staff, so that they can attend to major portions of the project and communicate with all of the concerned parties regarding the progress of the project. The expected cost is $1,920 in labor and an S&E cost of $160.00.

Page-2
4/12/96
8:29 PM
A Proposed WWW gateway to the
Government Printing Office (GPO) WAIS server
Carl Snow & Cary Kerr

Case 16   *GPO Access on the Web*—http://thorplus.lib.purdue.edu/gpo/

Contact: Carl E. Snow, Network Access Librarian, Purdue University Libraries (carl@thorplus.lib.purdue.edu) and Cary Kerr, Technical Information Systems Administrator (cary@lib.purdue.edu)

Purdue University's Government Documents Project is an example of a specialized electronic library, in fact it is an electric Government Documents Library. *GPO Access on the Web* was a patron-driven initiative. Carl Snow and Cary Kerr conceived of the project and implemented it. They had the full support of the Purdue University Libraries' administration.

They decided to go with the computer platform that was already available to them. This was a Sparc 10 running the SunOS 4.1.3—a Unix platform. Their computer was already running the NCSA HTTPd Webserver for Unix. They purchased two copies of an HTML editor software and 32 extra Megs of RAM for the Sparc 10. (A Sparc 10 with SunOS might cost between $10–20,000 depending on the specific system purchased. They estimate they spent $1,400 for equipment and software and

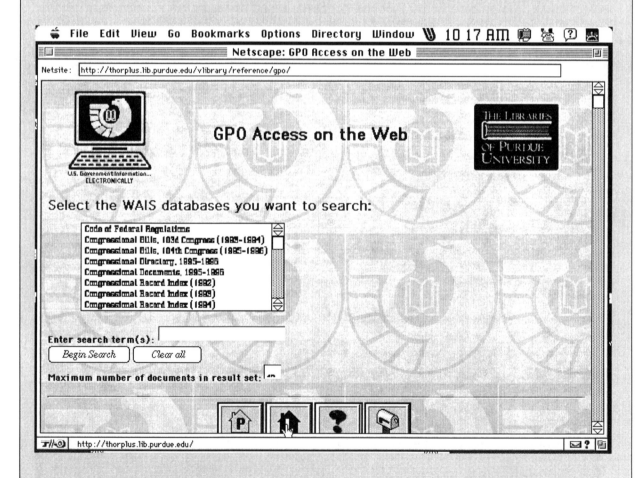

approximately $2,500 for their time for the project. They worked with existing staff in the technical support, management, and reference support for the project. Their total personnel commitment for ongoing maintenance and support of the GPO Access on the Web project is 3 people at less than 2 percent of their time or .8 hours per week. They plan to continue maintaining the project.

through its Web page is its catalog. This catalog uses DRA OPAC software. The link to it is actually a telnet connection to its catalog. Anyone is free to use it. The services available through the Web page for Cleveland Public Library cardholders also include more than 50 First Search databases (library cardholders must input their card number in order to access the databases).

In addition, a variety of freely available Internet resources is available to anyone connecting to Cleveland Public Library through the Internet. But even in organizing this collection the library focused on the information needs of its core user group. Internet resource categories include business, economics, and labor; children's literature; fine arts; travel; and other categories of information that are frequently needed by the users of a large urban public library.

Purdue University Libraries intended to make Government Printing Office databases, currently available through WAIS servers, easily available through Purdue Libraries' Web page. In other words, the libraries would offer an Internet extension of their government documents depository collection.

DO YOU HAVE PERSONNEL WHO ARE KNOWLEDGEABLE ENOUGH TO PRODUCE AND MAINTAIN AN ELECTRONIC LIBRARY BY MANAGING A GOPHER OR WORLD WIDE WEB SERVER?

The people who create the Web pages and gather and organize the links need only Internet searching skills, basic HTML skills, and Internet domain addressing knowledge. Depending on your choice of platform and Web server software you may need access to computer systems professionals. In both of the cases described in this chapter, the librarians had access to excellent existing platforms and to skilled systems people. These systems folks need to know how to manage the TCP/IP connections and how to install and maintain the server software. If you want or need to do this yourself, the Macintosh platform using MacHTTP server software is ideal.

Will you use Gopher or the World Wide Web?

There are very few reasons to use Gopher. The World Wide Web is a more accessible technology and is in some ways easier to use. The World Wide Web will also be more likely to let you expand or add services in the future.

What computer hardware and software is already available to you through your library, company, or organization?

Essentially, just do an inventory. Talk to your systems department if you have one.

What computer hardware and software will you need to purchase or otherwise acquire? What will it cost? How will you fund it? Where will you acquire it?

If you find you'll need to buy computers, establish an Internet connection, and obtain server software, you'll need to investigate costs and funding. Many states provide grant money for schools and public libraries for Internet projects. Contact your state or regional government agencies for information. If you have at least a basic Internet connection you can use Web search tools to search the Internet for grants and funding information.

You'll need to plan how much to request, and to establish contingencies for receiving less than your request. Chapter 1 describes hardware options and our opinions of them. Appendix A lists most of the software you'll need.

How much time do you estimate it will take to plan, implement, and maintain the electronic library?

The key issue with electronic libraries is time. Do you have someone who can spend time planning and implementing the electronic library? Cleveland Public Library made its project a priority of the Automation Systems Department, giving them all the time that those personnel could spare from their routine duties for planning, implementing, and maintaining the project. The library also received a commitment to ongoing expansion from its administration. For the Purdue University project, two librarians did the planning, and they had the assistance of student staff in implementing and maintaining their project. They estimated that three people spent less than 2 percent of their regular working hours on the project.

Obviously, the broader you intend your electronic collection to be, the more time it will require. A small, subject-focused electronic library collection might take only a few hours. For example, for a workshop for the Ohio Valley Area Libraries, "The Internet and Reference Service: Realities and Requirements," Diane created an "Internet Reference Collection." The focus enduser group was an imaginary community of public library users. The collection consisted of Internet resources that could be valuable in a small public library and could be used for ready reference. It took about two hours to plan and outline the entire project, another two hours to gather the resources, and two hours more to create a Web page to allow access to the "Internet Reference Collection." You can see it at http://phoenix.kent.edu/~dkovacs/ref.html, or e-mail diane@kovacs.com.

How many people will be needed to plan, implement, and then to maintain the service?

Once again this depends on the scope of what you want to do. One full-time person working with systems staff can do most projects. Larger projects like that of Cleveland Public Library might require the participation of entire departments.

IMPLEMENTATION

As you may have gathered, implementation of an electronic library requires time and attention. If you've thoughtfully made your decisions in the planning stage, implementation should be very routine. Basically, you must collect all the resources that you want to include in your electronic library, and either organize them with a

Gopher server or organize them on a Web page and put them on a World Wide Web server. Collecting the resources is a research task. HTML markup of the collected resources on a page is very simple; all that is required is a basic knowledge of HTML and an editor. There are many HTML editors; they all require knowledge of HTML be used effectively, but you could cobble something together with them even if you knew nothing of HTML. Gopher server organization requires knowledge of the basic directory and file commands on the operating system the Gopher server is running on.

MAINTENANCE

Once the electronic library is implemented it is usually feasible for anyone with basic computer skills to learn to maintain the service. Web pages are particularly easy because maintenance is primarily a clerical task. Running the Web server software might require skilled computer professionals, but if you're running a microcomputer Web server like MacHTTPd anyone with basic computer skills and knowledge of Macintosh networking can maintain it. In any case, maintenance will require regular checking of links to make sure they are current and working. It will also include ongoing collection and incorporation of new resources into your electronic library.

SUMMARY

An electronic library is a very ambitious project. It is complex and involved precisely because it recreates the physical library in virtual space. If librarians are to compete with other information professionals in the information age, then electronic libraries are a necessary step.

Chapter 5

Electronic Journals and Electronic Newsletters

Electronic journals and newsletters (e-journals and e-newsletters)—collectively called e-serials —are perhaps the most flexible Internet information product. The hardest thing about planning for them is to decide among all the available distribution options. Figure 5.1 outlines the questions to consider before you start an e-journal or e-newsletter.

PLANNING ELECTRONIC JOURNALS AND NEWSLETTERS

WILL YOU PRODUCE AN E-JOURNAL OR E-NEWSLETTER?

The key difference is style and content. E-journals will generally require much more work and will be more formally organized than e-newsletters. E-journals tend to be edited collections of articles by multiple authors; e-newsletters are more often written by one or a few people who write most of the articles for every issue. Some of you may wish to produce peer-reviewed, scholarly e-journals. Keep in mind that these will require the same intellectual, editorial, and clerical activities as print scholarly journals. The distribution mechanism and the media through which the articles are produced are the main differences.

Figure 5.1   Questions to Ask in Planning an Internet E-Journal or E-Newsletter

1. Will you produce an e-journal or e-newsletter?

2. For whom are you providing the e-journal or e-newsletter? What kind of Internet connectivity is available to your audience?

3. What kind of e-journal or e-newsletter will you produce? Why is it an important and/or appropriate information product for your library, school, company, or organization to provide?

4. Are you or others in your organization knowledgeable enough to produce and distribute an e-journal or e-newsletter?

5. What Internet distribution mechanism(s) will you use? Why?

6. What computer hardware and software is already available to you through your library, company, or organization?

7. What computer hardware and software will you need to purchase or otherwise acquire?

8. How much time do you estimate it will take to start up and maintain the e-journal or e-newsletter?

9. How many people will be needed to start up and maintain the e-journal or e-newsletter?

FOR WHOM ARE YOU PROVIDING THE E-JOURNAL OR E-NEWSLETTER? WHAT KIND OF INTERNET CONNECTIVITY IS AVAILABLE TO YOUR AUDIENCE?

This question is much less of concern for e-serials, as e-mail is all your readers will need. Anything else—such as Web archives or FTP sites—is frosting on the cake.

WHAT KIND OF E-JOURNAL OR E-NEWSLETTER WILL YOU PRODUCE? WHY IS IT AN IMPORTANT AND/OR APPROPRIATE INFORMATION PRODUCT FOR YOUR LIBRARY, SCHOOL, COMPANY OR ORGANIZATION TO PROVIDE?

These questions will have very different answers depending on your intentions. Basically you can choose some variation on the following:

Scholarly E-Journal. Someone will have to recruit authors and reviewers. An editor-in-chief must keep track of all the authors and reviewers and manage the communication between them. Figure 5.2 outlines the production and distribution activities involved in publishing the *Electronic Journal on Virtual Culture* as an example of the kind of work that may be involved.

Major work and time commitment for production will also be required. Even if your e-journal is not peer-reviewed, the editor-in-chief will have significant work in reading and editing the submissions.

Literary Collection. This type of e-serial publishes collected poetry, short stories, serial novels, or whatever literary works you want, and can be a really interesting (and fun) kind of project. The work involved requires reading and solicitation of submissions. There will, of course, also be much work involved in production.

Showcase for Local or Organizational Talent. This type of e-serial is really an e-newsletter. The best of this type are collections of articles on different topics by different people in an organization or even in a community. The same work requirements will be required for this as for the previous types.

News and Information Service. Carolyn Kotlas's *IAT Infobits* e-newsletter, described in Case 7, is this type of e-serial.

Figure 5.2   Production and Distribution of a Typical Issue of *The Electronic Journal on Virtual Culture* (http://rdz.stjohns.edu/ejvc/ejvc.html)

The Electronic Journal on Virtual Culture (EJVC) is a peer-reviewed e-journal, published quarterly through e-mail and the World Wide Web. EJVC has a standing editorial board made up of an Editor-in-Chief (EIC), the "Virtual Square" Opinions and Essays Section Editor, the "Cyberspace Monitor" News and Reviews Section Editor, and a group of supporting associate editors.

The editorial board consists of more than 40 scholars involved with research in the e-journal subject focus, which is the exploration of cultural and social aspects of the Internet. The peer-reviewers are initially drawn from the editorial board; Special issues and articles are reviewed by scholars chosen because of their own publication record in a particular area.

As for most print journals, the EIC's duties are to:

1. communicate calls for articles
2. coordinate special issue editors
3. identify peer-reviewers and make the articles received available to the peer reviewers
4. receive and file the reviews and make the reviews available to the editorial board
5. communicate the reviews and revisions to the author
6. receive revised articles and evaluate whether further revision is necessary
7. prepare title abstract listings for monthly LIBRES table of contents distribution
8. prepare and distribute the issue

As a rule, all calls for articles are made through e-mail distribution to discussion lists on topics related to the e-journal subject focus. Sometimes calls for articles are distributed on paper flyers at professional conferences. A common requirement of authors is that all articles be sent to the EIC through Internet e-mail. As they are already in electronic format, any reformatting is easily made. The EIC reads all articles for their initial appropriateness to the e-journal's subject focus, and communicates with the author confirmation of receipt of the article and plans for further review of the article.

All communication with authors takes place through Internet e-mail. For print journals, communication almost always takes place through regular postal mail. In our experience writing for print journals, it often takes weeks simply to communicate intent to review an article. EJVC can reasonably strive to notify an author within 48 hours of receipt of the article.

Reading each article and identifying peer-reviewers, however, can be very time-consuming. We've read articles that were so wordy and esoteric that none of us was sure what we were reading. In such cases the EIC sends the author e-mail asking him or her to rewrite it in common English as EJVC is a multidisciplinary e-journal and not all our readers would understand such specialized language. One particular rewritten article was one of our best published articles in the end.

Initial peer-reviewing is done by the editorial board members. All articles are reviewed without the author's name or e-mail address attached. To ensure that both the reviewers and the authors are anonymous, each prepublication article is made available on an FTP site and a Listserv fileserver. (Some of our editorial board members are in countries other than the United States, or are connecting to the Internet through commercial providers that have e-mail access only without FTP capability, so the Listserv fileserver is very useful.)

If no editorial board members feel qualified to review the article, the EIC does a literature search on the topic of the article and tries to locate qualified peer-reviewers. This usually happens for special issues with very esoteric topics; the special issue editor usually knows who the peer-reviewers should be. The EIC's tasks are to keep track of which article is from whom (sometimes a difficult task when we have several similar articles), to keep the reviewers focused on e-mailing their reviews back within the 30 days that we strive for, and to make sure that each article has at least three reviews.

Print journals often provide a form for reviewers to fill out. We simply ask our reviewers to answer some set questions about the article and recommend revisions, rejection, or publication. So far we have had only a couple of articles go through more than two revisions before they were accepted. Several times authors disagreed with the revisions and withdrew their articles. We have rejected several articles that were inappropriate or were just badly researched. The EIC communicates with the authors via e-mail any recommended revisions and the deadlines for making those revisions if the article is conditionally accepted for publication.

This review process is almost exactly what the print journal EIC does. The differences are the mechanisms for communicating with the authors and reviewers. The cost is much lower because the transfer of the articles and reviews and communications take place through e-mail rather than paper mail.

The intellectual production process is virtually the same between the print and the electronic journal. The production process is becoming more similar as many publishers are asking authors to send their articles on a diskette. All formatting and revisions are done electronically—no retyping is ever required. The format is ASCII text which can be converted to any other format very easily if necessary.

Distribution is the aspect that is the most different. When a print journal is distributed, it must be printed, collated, proofed, and finally mailed out to subscribers. For the electronic journal, the journal is simply formatted and proofed and the table of contents is e-mailed to subscribers. The cost of distribution in the print environment is a major part of the cost of publication, the cost of distribution of an e-journal is negligible.

Case 17 _IAT Infobits_—http://www.iat.unc.edu/infobits/infobits.html or send email to listserv@unc.edu with the message: subscribe infobits Yourfirstname Yourlastname

_Contact: Carolyn Kotlas, Director, Institute for Academic Technology Library, University of North Carolina–Chapel Hill (carolyn_kotlas@unc.edu)_

IAT Infobits is an electronic newsletter (e-newsletter). Carolyn Kotlas conceived of _Infobits_ as a way of extending the Institute for Academic Technology Library (IAT) services and resources to other people at the University of North Carolina–Chapel Hill. Her supervisor, Dr. William Graves, Director of IAT, suggested she use another e-journal, _Edupage_, as a model for format and general content.

The IAT library is a one-professional library—all activities are initiated and implemented by that one professional. Carolyn performed all the information gathering, writing, and editing. She did get some help with proofreading from the IAT's publications editor. Although Carolyn did not write a project plan, she did have a clear goal in mind for the e-newsletter. That was to provide faculty and computer support staff at UNC-CH up-to-date simply written, information on educational/instructional technologies, and other resources that might encourage and assist them in teaching with new technologies. _Infobits_ proved so successful that IAT began distributing it to subscribers outside the UNC-CH system.

In order to keep her time organized, Carolyn publishes the e-newsletter once a month at around the same time. She also keeps the length of each issue equivalent to one double-sided page of text.

The only distribution option that seemed practical initially was through Listserv. IAT is not physically located on the UNC-CH campus so they were prepared to distribute to their local end users via the Internet. They do make printed copies to pass out at workshops and for IAT visitors. As with the _PACS Review_, _Infobits_ was published using the software and hardware already available to IAT. Initial costs were essentially zero, the e-newsletter was published as part of Carolyn Kotlas' job description.

Currently two people maintain the e-newsletter. Carolyn estimates that she spends 10–12 hours per month collecting and verifying information, writing articles, and distributing the e-newsletter. Recently she also began spending about 30 minutes per month formatting an HTML version for a Web page distribution. She estimates she spends 2 hours per month handling subscription requests and subcriber problems. The IAT publications editor helps out with 45 minutes each month proofreading the e-newsletter before it is distributed.

Infobits continues to be very popular. Recently, the UNC campus upgraded their hardware and installed Listproc. *Infobits* is now distributed using Listproc. Carolyn feels that e-mail distribution of ASCII text is the most efficient way of serving a majority of end users. The Web page supplements the distribution and provides a straightforward way of archiving.

ARE YOU OR OTHERS IN YOUR ORGANIZATION KNOWLEDGEABLE ENOUGH TO PRODUCE AND DISTRIBUTE AN E-JOURNAL OR E-NEWSLETTER?

You or others that you work with must know how to use e-mail very well—how to type, read, edit, and copyedit. You don't need to know a great deal about the Internet. When you need to learn to use the e-mail distribution software, (Listserv, Listproc, or Majordomo, for example) you can retrieve the documentation on the Internet. James Milles's "Discussion Lists: Mail List Manager Commands" (http://lawlib.slu.edu/training/mailser.htm) is the best of what's available (see Appendix B for others).

WHAT INTERNET DISTRIBUTION MECHANISM(S) WILL YOU USE? WHY?

E-mail is ideal for distributing e-serials directly to readers. You can distribute the e-serial directly to anyone who wants to receive it. You can also archive the e-serial on a Web server and e-mail tables of contents or simply announcements of a new issue. FTP or Gopher servers are also archiving possibilities, but Web servers are clearly superior—the Web is very widely used, and with it you can even provide the e-serial in a nicely formatted style.

WHAT COMPUTER HARDWARE AND SOFTWARE IS ALREADY AVAILABLE TO YOU THROUGH YOUR LIBRARY, COMPANY, OR ORGANIZATION?

As both case descriptions in this chapter indicate, many university and college libraries will have access to computers running popular e-mail mailing list management software. Contact anyone in your organization who will know what is locally available to you. Don't overlook your Internet service provider. Many Internet service providers run Listerv, Listproc, Majordomo, or other mailing list software that you might be able to use.

WHAT COMPUTER HARDWARE AND SOFTWARE WILL YOU NEED TO PURCHASE OR OTHERWISE ACQUIRE?

Appendix A lists sources for the major mailing list software. There is a licensing fee associated with all but Majordomo. If you do not already have a computer system available, it might be a wise idea to review the software and then choose the computer system that will work with that software.

You might also investigate local universities. Many will let local libraries use their mailing list management software either for a small fee or as part of their community support requirements. It can't hurt to ask and you might be pleasantly surprised by the response.

HOW MUCH TIME DO YOU ESTIMATE IT WILL TAKE TO START UP AND MAINTAIN THE E-JOURNAL OR E-NEWSLETTER?

One good thing about e-serials is that, aside from the time to plan the project, each issue will take about the same amount of time to produce and distribute. As Carolyn Kotlas notes in Case 7, the e-newsletter can take 10 to 12 hours per month for research, writing, and verification. She spends about an hour every month in formatting the Web archive and in e-mail distribution. Charles Bailey (see Case 18) doesn't keep track of his time or the time of other people who work on *The Public-Access Computer Systems Review*. From our experience, a scholarly e-journal takes an average of 20 hours per issue in soliciting and reviewing articles, production, and distribution for the editor-in-chief. That doesn't take into account the time taken by reviewers and contributers.

HOW MANY PEOPLE WILL BE NEEDED TO START UP AND MAINTAIN THE E-JOURNAL OR E-NEWSLETTER?

Think of this in terms of how much time your library will want to invest in the project. A team approach means that less time is required for each individual, but more time might be required for coordination of effort.

Case 18   *The Public-Access Computer Systems Review* **http://info.lib.uh.edu/ pacsrev.html or send e-mail to listserv@uhupvm1.uh.edu with the message: subscribe PACS-P Yourfirstname Yourlastname**

Contact: Charles Bailey, Assistant Director for Systems, University of Houston Libraries (cbailey@uh.edu)

The Public-Access Computer Systems Review (PACS Review) was the first library/librarian-related electronic journal published on the Internet. Charles Bailey came up with the idea and posted a message to PACS-L@uhupvm1.uh.edu. By September 1989 he had gathered an editorial board and begun planning. The editorial board used a special closed discussion list for its communications. Charles and the editorial board did not draft a written plan, although they thoroughly discussed their ideas through e-mail to each other. They conceived of *PACS Review* as an experiment to test the viability of scholarly electronic journals. For more background you can read Charles Bailey's articles listed in the bibliography.

Initially, they intended the e-journal to be distributed and archived using the Revised Listserv software. University Houston had the software already installed on an existing

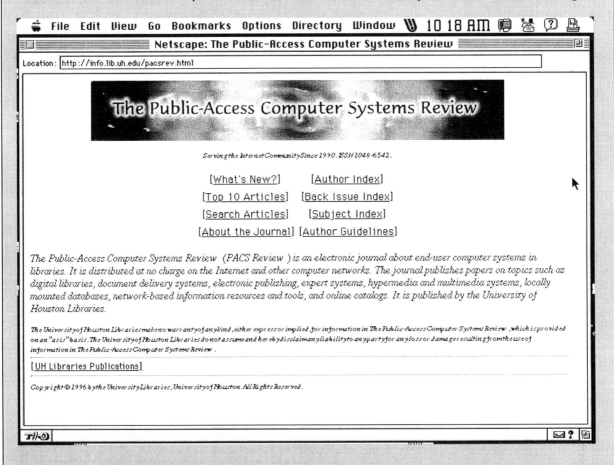

AS/9000 IBM-compatible mainframe running the VM/CMS operating system. They did not need to purchase any hardware or software to support production and distribution of the *PACS Review*.

Charles Bailey used regular working hours and many hours of his own time at home to edit the e-journal. In the early days of the journal, he was the only staff member at University of Houston Libraries working on the project; Mike Ridley, then of McMaster University, was the Associate Editor. They worked entirely through e-mail. Neither required training as they were already experienced Listserv listowners.

Currently, Charles works with Dana Rooks and Ann Thornton at University of Houston, and Leslie Dillon at OCLC to maintain *PACS Review* as one of the premier journals for information and library science. They don't keep records of the time they spend but they do have the support of University of Houston Libraries to spend appropriate work hours on the project.

At present, the *PACS Review* is published and archived through Listserv and Gopher, as well as the World Wide Web. The Listserv and Gopher versions are ASCII text, and of course the Web version is HTMLed.

IMPLEMENTATION

Once you've planned your e-serial it is time to obtain an International Standard Serial Number (ISSN)—a unique identifier for every serial. The ISSN is used in many online bibliographic databases and in interlibrary loan transactions to identify the needed serial and expedite requests. It will also get your e-serial cataloged by the Library of Congress and therefore into databases like OCLC and RLIN. To obtain an ISSN, U.S. publishers can connect to http://lcweb.loc.gov or contact the National Serials Data Program, Library of Congress, Washington, D.C. 20540 (202–707–6452). Non-U.S. publishers should contact the International Serials Data System International Center, 20 rue Bachaumont, 75002 Paris, France (1) 42.36.73.81.

You may also want to contact appropriate indexing and abstracting services (such as, ERIC, Psychological Abstracts, or MLA International Bibliography). Coverage in such indexes will help endusers find articles and locate Internet resources for their information need. (Note that it can be a trial for traditional interlibrary loan services to receive this kind of request. During 1995, EJVC's editor-in-chief received six ILL requests for articles in the e-journal. She telephoned the ILL requesters and explained to them how to retrieve the articles from the Internet archives.)

The same intellectual, editing, and clerical tasks required for paper journals and newsletters are required for e-serials. For an e-journal, an editorial board and people willing to work as editors, copyeditors, and typists are also required. E-newsletters might not need a complex support system like an editorial board but you'll still need writers, editors, copyeditors, and typists. Someone must write, collect, and screen articles and other pieces for the e-serial. Then someone must review, revise, and edit the pieces. Only then are you ready to format the pieces into a unit and distribute it.

The e-serial differs from the paper journal or newsletter in its format and its distribution mechanisms. The format of an e-serial will be in electronic text—for example ASCII text, an HTML document, some other kind of text format like Postscript, or some proprietary word-processing format—that you decided on in the planning phase. The distribution mechanisms will also be decided in the planning stage. If you are e-mailing tables of contents, put the entire e-serial on the server and test retrieval—before you e-mail the table of contents or announcement. If you've chosen a Listserv, Listproc, Majordomo, or another kind of managed e-mail distribution, you'll simply need to mail the table of contents or announcement to the group address and your job is done until the next issue.

MAINTENANCE

Maintenance of an e-serial requires the same kind of intellectual, editorial, and clerical activities as implementation. In fact, for every issue, you will implement all over again; it really never gets any easier as time goes by. The same work that goes into the first issue will go into every subsequent issue. Fortunately, you'll only have to plan everything once. You might find as time passes, however, that your e-serial needs some fine-tuning, either in format, content, or even frequency of distribution. For example, EJVC started as an experiment in distributing peer-reviewed articles as they were accepted. We soon found that a publication schedule was necessary for everyone involved, to coordinate our efforts and make plans.

SUMMARY

The e-serial is the future of serials publication. Libraries are increasingly challenged to supply these products to their endusers and to archive the scholarly record for future researchers. In that process we must be proactive. One aspect of librarians publishing e-journals is that we can learn all the ins and outs of the process, thereby gaining knowledge that will help us teach each other to provide access for our endusers to e-serials produced by commercial and scholarly vendors—today and in the future.

Chapter 6

Afterword and One Last Kind of Internet Application

Internet training provided by libraries for their staff or endusers is becoming increasingly common. Although some might argue that Internet training is beyond the scope of library services, it is almost beyond debate in many settings. Many librarians realize that Internet training is the bibliographic instruction—or rather the "research instruction"—of our future. That future is definitely here.

Offering or at least marketing traditional library services through the Internet is also something we should be starting to do. The importance of traditional library services in the Internet context, we believe, is that this is where libraries are headed. At the same time, librarians must be proactive in convincing administrators in all sorts of organizations that our services are not replaceable by the Internet . . . but we've got to prove it. Furthermore, we must overcome the belief held by many librarians that the library is merely the book collection. That belief keeps them from realizing that the library is more than just a storage space and is in fact the sum of all the services, including research services and organizing the storage space. Unfortunately, we've vacated that role to others where the Internet is concerned.

The creation of electronic libraries is a tremendous stride toward staking out our territory on the Internet. It means organizing Internet "storage space" or archives and being a valuable presence on the Internet. It is not true that the Internet is a passing fad; it is true that the Internet is where more and more of our endusers are looking to fill their information needs.

There is less justification for producing an e-serial than there is for producing the previously discussed information products. Nevertheless, although it might take another 10 or 15 years, the Internet will in the end be the medium through which most publishers produce and distribute information products. If your library already produces a newsletter or magazine, the Internet production and distribution will save you money over print production and postal or even campus mail distribution costs. The Internet is also a medium through which many endusers want to receive their serials. More than that, producing something as familiar as a serial on the Internet can provide librarians with a clearer understanding of the mechanics of the Internet and give them the insight they'll need to archive and organize other e-serials.

There is an additional kind of Internet information product that none of the previous chapters have dealt with directly: the reference tool, bibliography, directory, or index produced by a library and published on the Internet for the benefit of the general public. For example, the Cleveland Public Libraries have produced the *Cleveland News Index* as a print publication since the 1930s (with some interruptions). It is an index to the *Cleveland Plain Dealer* and several other Cleveland area newspapers. When the Cleveland Public Libraries' Electronic Library was created, it included a searchable database version of the *Cleveland News Index*.

The *Directory of Scholarly and Professional E-Conferences* (see Figure 6.1) is another example of such a product. It is also unique among the applications described in this book because it was never and is not currently a product of a library. It is a product of librarians from different libraries, in different states—and currently in different countries.

The original idea in the fall of 1990 was to produce an information product that would demonstrate to Internet users that librarians were and could be valuable assets on the Internet. Although an annual print version is published by the Association of Research Libraries under the title *Directory of Electronic Journals, Newsletters and Academic Discussion Lists,* the electronic version is freely available on the Internet (with the proviso that copyright is maintained by the Directory Team).

The directory is a compilation and indexing of e-conferences (an umbrella term for Listserv, Comserve, Mailbase, Mailserv, Major-

Figure 6.1	**10th Revision, *Directory of Scholarly and Professional E-Conferences* (Previously titled: 10th Revision, *Directory of Scholarly E-Conferences*)**

Contents
1. Fair Use Guidelines
2. Scope of the Directory
3. The Directory Team
4. Acknowledgements
5. How to Access or Retrieve the Directory of Scholarly and Professional E-Conferences
6. Generic Subscription Instructions
7. Generic Archives Access Instructions

1. Fair Use Guidelines

Single copies of this directory from its networked sources, or of specific entries from their networked sources, may be made for internal purposes, personal use, or study by an individual, an individual library, or an educational or research institution. The Association of Research Libraries has sole right to produce a print edition. The directory or its contents may not be otherwise reproduced or republished in excerpt or entirety, in print or electronic form, without permission from Diane K. Kovacs, diane@kovacs.com.

2. Scope of the Directory

This directory contains descriptions of electronic conferences (e-conferences) on topics of interest to scholars and professionals for use in their scholarly, pedagological, and professional activities.

E-conference is the umbrella term that includes discussion lists, Internet interest groups, Usenet newsgroups, forums,etc. Since the 9th revision we have begun including text-based virtual reality systems, known as MUDs, MOOs, MUCKs, MUSHs, etc., that are primarily for scholarly, pedagogical, or professional activities.

The e-conferences in this directory are all accessible via Internet services including e-mail, Usenet News Readers, telnet, Gopher, or WWW.

We have used our own judgment in deciding what is of scholarly, pedagological, or professional interest, but always consider any advice or argument about our decisions. We have placed the entries into categories by deciding the *dominant* academic subject area of the electronic conference.

Where possible, the information in each record has been checked for currency and accuracy by contacting the moderators or other contact person.

We chose the term *moderator* as the umbrella term to describe: contact person, coordinator, listowner, editor, moderator, etc.; in other words the Human in Charge.

Topic descriptions are taken in whole or part from the descriptions provided by each moderator.

The basic fields are described as follows:

Discussion Name:	The name of the group; the listname.
Topic:	Short description of the group; usually in the listowner's words.
Subscription Address:	This is the address to send your subscription and signoff messages to.
Moderated?	Does some human screen messages either by editing or by monitoring? Is the list set to private?
Archives:	Are there archives? Where?
Contact Address:	The moderator; who to contact if you have questions.
Submission Address:	Where to send your contributions to the group's discussion.
Keywords:	Words to enhance retrieval of an entry in search systems.
VR:	The version and cutoff date for entries in this version.

3. The Directory Team

Diane Kovacs, Editor-in-Chief diane@kovacs.com
  • Education
  • Biological and Medical Sciences
  • Jobs, Employment, Placement Services and Programs
  • Computer Science
  • Physical Sciences

Leela Balraj lbalraj@kentvm.kent.edu
  • History
  • Law, Criminology, Justice
  • Political Science and Politics
  • Business
  • Economics
  • Human Resources and Industrial Psychology

Gladys Bell gbell@kentvm.kent.edu
  • Anthropology and Archaeology
  • Geography and Misc. Regional and Individual Country Studies
  • Latin American Studies
  • Social Activism
  • Sociology and Demography
  • Gender and Women's Studies

Paul Fehrmann pfehrman@kentvm.kent.edu
  • Philosophy and Ethics
  • Psychology

Martha Fleming mkf@po.cwru.edu
- Communication Studies
- Journalism
- Religious Studies

Lydia Gamble lgamble@kentvm.kent.edu
- Humanities (Comparative and Interdisciplinary)
- Languages
- Linguistics and Text Analysis
- Literature
- Writing

Kara Robinson krobinso@kentvm.kent.edu
- Art, Architecture, and Urban Design
- Library and Information Science
- Music
- Physical Education, Recreation, and Dance
- Popular Culture
- Publishing and Related Issues
- Theater, Film, and Television

Dennis Viehland d.viehland@massey.ac.nz
- Information Systems

4. Acknowledgements

Thank you to Marty Hoag, Listowner of New-List, for providing the archives of New-List as a clearinghouse for much of the e-mail–based discussion list information. Special thank you to David Hartland, NISP/Mailbase Project, Computing Service, The University, Newcastle-upon-Tyne, for information on 235 of the United Kingdom MAILBASE e-conferences. Thank you also to Teri Harrison for updating and providing information on the COMSERVE conferences, Pedro Saizar for providing information on Latin American Studies electronic conferences, Joseph Van Zwaren for providing Israeli electronic conference information, Joan Korenman for providing information on Women's Studies conferences, and Jean Schneider for confirming European e-conferences. Thank you very sincerely to all the individuals who contributed conference names, information, and feedback about conference statuses. Any errors are the responsibility of the compilers of each section. If you can provide corrections or additional information about any of these electronic conferences, please contact the Directory Team member responsible for that area or:

Diane Kovacs, Editor-in-Chief diane@kovacs.com

5. How to Access or Retrieve the *Directory of Scholarly and Professional E-Conferences*

An annual print version is published by the Association of Research Libraries. Contact the Publication Department pubs@cni.org for information.

WWW Homepage:
MIDNet Site
http://www.n2h2.com/KOVACS
Contact: Paul Kramer paul@n2h2.com

Gopher access:
University of Saskatchewan
Contact: Earl Fogel earl.fogel@usask.ca
gopher://gopher.usask.ca/1/Computing/Internet
Information/Directory of Scholarly Electronic Conferences

E-mail:
How to retrieve files from the LISTSERV@LISTSERV.KENT.EDU

1. Send an e-mail message addressed to LISTSERV@LISTSERV.KENT.EDU.
2. Leave the subject and other info lines blank.
3. The message must read: GET Filename Filetype (e.g., ACADLIST ANTHRO).
4. If you need assistance receiving, etc., contact your local Computer Services people.

Files Available

ACADLIST.ACTIVIST	=	Social Activism
ACADLIST.ANTHRO	=	Anthropology, Cross Cultural Studies, and Archaeology
ACADLIST.ART	=	Art, Architecture, and Urban Design
ACADLIST.ASTRONOM	=	Astronomy
ACADLIST.BIOLOGY	=	Genetics, General Biology/Biophysics/Biochemistry
ACADLIST.BOTANY	=	Botany/Horticulture
ACADLIST.BUSECON	=	Business, Accounting, Finance, and Marketing and Economics
	=	Human Resources and Industrial Psychology
ACADLIST.CHEMIST	=	Chemistry, Chemical Engineering, and Materials Research
ACADLIST.COMMJOUR	=	Communication and Journalism
ACADLIST.COMPENG	=	Computer Engineering, Software Engineering
ACADLIST.COMPSEC	=	Computer Security
ACADLIST.COMPRES	=	Computer Science Research: Artificial Intelligence, Expert Systems, Virtual Reality
	=	Computer Science Research: Computer Standards (Official and De Facto)
	=	Computer Science Research: General Academic
ACADLIST.COMPSYS	=	Computer Systems: Network Administration
	=	Computer Systems: System Administration

	=	Computer Systems: Training and User Support
ACADLIST.COMPMISC	=	Miscellaneous Computer-Related
	=	Public Domain and Publically Supported Software
ACADLIST.COMPPRGM	=	Programming Languages and Programming
ACADLIST.COMPSOC	=	Social, Cultural, and Political Aspects of Computing
ACADLIST.EDUC	=	Education: Computer-Assisted Instruction/Educational Technology
	=	Education: Educational Research (general), Grants and Funding
	=	Education: Higher, Adult and Continuing Education
	=	Education: Primary, Secondary (K-12), Vocational and Technical
	=	Education: Miscellaneous Education, Alumni and Student Groups
	=	Education: Special Education, Developmental Disabilities, Physical Disabilities and ADA (Americans with Disabilities Act)
ACADLIST.ENGINEER	=	Engineering and Technology General and Transportation Engineering
ACADLIST.FUTURE	=	Futurology/Future Studies
ACADLIST.ENVIRON	=	Ecology and Environmental Studies
ACADLIST.GEOGRAPH	=	Geography and Miscellaneous Regional and Individual Country Studies
ACADLIST.GEOLOGY	=	Geology and Paleontology
ACADLIST.HISTORY	=	History
ACADLIST.HUMGEN	=	Humanities (Comparative and Interdisciplinary)
ACADLIST.INFORETR	=	Information Retrieval
ACADLIST.INFOSYS	=	Information Systems
ACADLIST.INTERNET	=	Internet Tools and Resources
ACADLIST.JOBS	=	Jobs, Employment, Placement Services and Programs
ACADLIST.LANG	=	Languages
ACADLIST.LATAM	=	Latin American Studies
ACADLIST.LAW	=	Law, Criminology, Justice
ACADLIST.LIBRARY	=	Library and Information Science
ACADLIST.LING	=	Linguistics and Text Analysis
ACADLIST.LIT	=	Literature
	=	Writing
ACADLIST.MATH	=	Mathematics and Statistics
ACADLIST.MEDICAL	=	Medical Practice/Nursing/Medical Personnel/Patients and Medical Sciences/Research
ACADLIST.METEOR	=	Weather and Meteorology
ACADLIST.MIL	=	Military Science

ACADLIST.MUSIC	= Music
ACADLIST.PERD	= Physical Education, Recreation, and Dance
ACADLIST.PHILOS	= Philosophy and Ethics
ACADLIST.PHYSICS	= Physics
ACADLIST.POLITICS	= Political Science and Politics
ACADLIST.POPULAR	= Theater, Film and Television, and Popular Culture
ACADLIST.PSYCH	= Psychology and Psychiatry
ACADLIST.PUBLISH	= Publishing and Related Issues
ACADLIST.RELIG	= Religious Studies
ACADLIST.SCIENCE	= Science and Technology (Miscellaneous)
ACADLIST.SOCIOLOG	= Sociology and Demography
ACADLIST.VETZOO	= Agriculture, Veterinary Science, and Zoology
ACADLIST.WOMEN	= Women's Studies/Gender Studies

6. Generic Subscription Instructions

LISTSERV, COMSERVE, LISTPROC, MAILBASE, MAILSERV

To subscribe to a LISTSERV (both Unix and IBM/VM LSOFT LISTSERV software is in use) COMSERVE, LISTPROC, MAILBASE, or MAILSERV, e-mail distributed e-conference, send an e-mail message addressed to the e-mail address provided in the "Subscription Address" field. Leave the subject line blank. The text of the message *must* read:

SUBSCRIBE LISTNAME Yourfirstname Yourlastname Your Institution

LISTNAME means the name of the list (e.g., if the List Name field says LIBREF-L, the LISTNAME is LIBREF-L).

Do not include any other text and *leave the subject line blank* as this is being read by a computer program and not a person. The program just won't understand and will bounce back your command if it is not worded as specified above.

-REQUEST Addresses

To subscribe to e-conferences with a -REQUEST address, send an e-mail message to list-REQUEST@host (e.g., SOC-CULTURE-GREEK-REQUEST@CS.WISC.EDU). Use the same basic directions as with the Listserv software. The -REQUEST address gets you to the Coordinator, rather than to the membership of the entire e-conference. Please look carefully at the entry for each list you are interested in, to see if a -REQUEST address has been provided. Include your name, address, and institutional affiliation in your message.

USENET NEWSGROUPS

Usenet Newsgroups are generally accessed by typing "RN" or "NN" at the shell prompt, ready screen, or $ prompt on your e-mail account. Check with your Computer Services people to find out what the local availability and procedures are for access to Usenet Newsgroups.

MAJORDOMO

Send e-mail to the majordomo@site address. The text of the message should be:

subscribe listname youremailaddress

Subscription directions for other types of discussions
are included with individual entries.

See also a fine publication titled: "Discussion Lists: Mail List Manager Commands" by James Milles, Saint Louis University Law Library millesjg@sluvca.slu.edu.

7. Generic Archives Access Instructions

Archives are available for many discussions. On LISTSERV, COMSERVE, MAILSERV, and MAILBASE to receive a list of files available from a server send the command:

INDEX LISTNAME to SERVER@NODEID

You can then send the message:

GET Filename Filetype

to the SERVER@NODEID. (SERVER means LISTSERV or COMSERVE or MAILBASE or MAILSERV or whatever; NODEID means the site of the server which runs the e-conference.)

It is also possible to search Bitnet LISTSERV and COMSERVE discussion archives for items of particular interest to you. For details on archives searching:
For LISTSERV send the message:

INFO DATABASE

to a LISTSERV of your choice (e.g., LISTSERV@PSUVM).
For COMSERVE send the message:

HELPFILE

to Comserve@cios.llc.rpi.edu.

Some discussions maintain archives available via anonymous FTP. This is noted where available. Some archives are maintained on other types of Internet server, e.g., GOPHER and WWW. Use the URL provided to connect to those archive sites.

When in doubt use the Contact Address.

domo, Listproc, and manually managed e-mail discussions; Usenet newsgroups, MUDs, MOOs, and the like; and some Web pages). The key criterion for inclusion is that each entry be a global, permanent discussion that takes place on the Internet between people interested in a topic that is scholarly or professional. The directory team evaluates and screens submissions so that people who want to use the Internet discussions for their research, teaching, and professional activities are not subjected to "junk." When last we counted, the directory was available at or through nearly 1,000 sites worldwide.

The directory is a uniquely Internet information product; the information is compiled from Internet sources—including Internet users—and is published on the Internet. Since the directory began, many similar products have been produced both by librarians and others. This phenomenon indicates to us that the Internet is at its core a powerful information archive and information distribution medium.

An article in the *Electronic Journal on Virtual Culture* (http://rdz.stjohns.edu/ejvc/ejvc.html) provides the history of the directory project from 1991 to 1993. The current directory team and official URLs for accessing the *Directory of Scholarly and Professional E-Conferences* are listed in Figure 6.1.

Our official Web site uses a CGI search engine programmed in Perl. Many such database projects are on the Web—making databases of all kinds searchable through a Web page increasingly easier. First WAIS (for example, the Purdue project, Case 16 in Chapter 4) and now CGI and Java scripts are available that can be used to link Web pages to databases (see Appendix B for some useful links). Also, most commercial Web server software now supports various methods of access to commercial and free databases.

Projects like those described in this book, and specifically projects like the *Directory of Scholarly and Professional E-Conferences*, are the future of our profession. Librarians' domain has expanded through time from clay tablets to papyrus scrolls, to printed books to online catalogs, to databases, to CD-ROMS; and now our domain is the Internet. These publication media represent increasingly sophisticated methods of permanently organizing and communicating information. As always, it is the duty of librarians to organize, catalog, and make this information more readily available to those who need it.

Appendix A

Selected Internet Server and Client Software Distributions on the Internet (organized by computer platform)

Note: Some of these software distributions also contain tutorials for installing and using the software; where appropriate, these are sometimes also listed in Appendix B.

Many Web servers are not included here. These two sites are excellent places to find more up-to-date information about Web software, including reviews, prices, and functionality.

WebCompare Web Servers Comparisons
http://www.proper.com/www/servers-chart.html
Overview of Web server software with reviews and basic functionalities.

World Wide Web Server Software Meta Resource List
http://www.comvista.com/us/lea/servers.html
Attempt to create a comprehensive list of available Web server software. Compiled by Lea Silk (lsilk@comvista.com).

UNIX

Apache Web Server
http://www.apache.org/
  Unix Web server

Commerce Builder Web Server
http://www.ifact.com/ifact/inet.htm
  Windows NT and Unix Web Server.

Gopher Software Distribution for Unix
ftp://boombox.micro.umn.edu:/pub/gopher
gopher://boombox.micro.umn.edu/1/gopher
  Gopher server and client software for Unix platforms.

LISTPROC or the Unix Listserver (also known, as of version 6.0a, as ListProcessor)
ftp://cs.bu.edu/pub/listserv
  Listproc was written by Anastasios Kotsikonas. It has very similar functionality to the L-Soft, or Revised, Listserv software but runs only on Unix computers.

Listserv (L-Soft Listserv)
http://www.lsoft.com
ftp://ftp.lsoft.com
gopher://gopher.lsoft.com
(Send e-mail to lsv-info@bitnic.educom.org.)
  The L-Soft Listserv, or Revised Listserv, is the original Listserv software written by Eric Thomas. It is available for Unix, IBM/VM/CMS, VAX/VMS, and Windows NT.

MAJORDOMO
ftp://FTP.GreatCircle.COM/pub/majordomo
  Majordomo is Unix-based e-mail distribution management software for discussion lists and electronic journals. Its development emerged from discussions of the Internet Engineering Task Force Listserv Working Group. It functions similarly to other Listserv-like software in that commands sent as the text of e-mail messages are received by the Majordomo software and processed. Majordomo was written by Brent Chapman (brent@GreatCircle.COM).

NCSA HTTPd

http://hoohoo.ncsa.uiuc.edu/
ftp://ftp.ncsa.uiuc.edu/Web

HTTPd Web server software for Windows, Windows NT, and Unix.

Netscape Web Servers

http://home.netscape.com/

Netscape's Enterprise, FastTrack, and other commercial Web Servers.

TCP/IP and Related Software

ftp://ftp.ncsa.uiuc.edu
ftp://ftp.utas.edu.au
gopher://ici.proper.com
(Pick the directory for your type of computer.)

TCP/IP–related software for Macintosh, DOS, Windows, and Unix. Includes WWW clients and servers, Winsock applications, NCSA telnet, graphics viewing software, sound applications, and WAIS and Archie clients software.

WAIS Server and Client Software

ftp://think.com/wais

For Macintosh, and lots of different Unix.

WebSite

http://software.ora.com/download/
Windows Web server by O'Reilly & Associates.

MACINTOSH

CL-HTTP: Common Lisp Hypermedia Server

http://www.ai.mit.edu/projects/iiip/doc/cl-http/home-page.html

Web server software by John C. Mallery for Macintosh and Windows.

FTPd

ftp://sumex-aim.stanford.edu/info-mac/comm/tcp

FTP server software for Macintosh written by Peter Lewis. It will also run as a Gopher server.

Gopher Surfer

ftp://boombox.micro.umn.edu/pub/gopher/Mac_server/
gopher://boombox.micro.umn.edu/1/gopher

Gopher server software available for both 68k and Power Macs. Also Gopher client software for Macs.

httpd4Mac Home page

http://sodium.ch.man.ac.uk/pages/httpd4Mac/home.html

Macintosh Web server software.

InterServer Publisher

http://www.intercon.com/newpi/InterServerP.html

Macintosh Web server software by InterCon.

MacHTTP

ftp://oac.hsc.uth.tmc.edu/public/mac/MacHTTP

Macintosh Web server written by Chuck Shotton. It is very powerful, has built-in security, and is an excellent overall Web server. WebStar was developed from this program.

Macjordomo: A Macintosh Listserver!

http://leuca.med.cornell.edu/Macjordomo

Mailing list management software for the Macintosh 68k and PowerPCs.

MacPPP

ftp://ftp.merit.edu/internet.tools/ppp/mac/

Macintosh Point to Point Protocol (PPP) software for Macintosh PPP dial-up connections. Requires MacTCP.

NCSA Telnet

ftp://ftp.ncsa.uiuc.edu/Mac/Telnet

Telnet connection software for Macintosh TCP/IP and related software
ftp://ftp.ncsa.uiuc.edu
ftp://ftp.utas.edu.au
gopher://ici.proper.com
(Pick the directory for your type of computer.)

NetAlly

http://www.delphic.com/netally.html

Macintosh Web server software by Delphic Software, Inc.

NetPresenz
ftp://redback.cs.uwa.edu.au/others/peterlewis/home-page.html
   Macintosh Web server software by Peter Lewis.

Netwings
http://netwings.com/nest.html
   Macintosh Web server software by Netwings Corporation.

NovaServer 4
http://www.resnova.com/product/
   Web server software (for 4D database system) by ResNova for Macintosh and Windows.

TCP/IP and Related Software
ftp://ftp.ncsa.uiuc.edu
ftp://ftp.utas.edu.au
gopher://ici.proper.com
(Pick the directory for your type of computer.)
   TCP/IP–related software for Macintosh, DOS, Windows, and Unix. Includes WWW clients and servers, Winsock applications, NCSA telnet, graphics viewing software, sound applications, and WAIS and Archie clients software.

TeleFinder BBS
http://www.spiderisland.com/
   Web server software by Spider Island Software for Macintosh and Windows.

WAIS Server and Client Software
ftp://think.com/wais
   For Macintosh, and lots of different Unix.

Webink Lite
http://www.webink.com/
   Macintosh Web server software by Webink.

WebStar by StarNine Technologies
http://www.starnine.com/
   One of the best Macintosh Web server software programs.

IBM/VM/CMS

Gopher Software Distribution for VM/CMS

ftp://boombox.micro.umn.edu:/pub/gopher
gopher://boombox.micro.umn.edu/1/gopher
   Gopher server and client software for IBM/VM/CMS platforms.

Listserv (L-Soft Listserv)

ftp://ftp.lsoft.com - gopher://gopher.lsoft.com
(Send e-mail to lsv-info@bitnic.educom.org.)
   The LSoft Listserv or Revised Listserv is the original Listserv software written by Eric Thomas. It is available for Unix, IBM/VM/CMS, VAX/VMS, and Windows NT.

WebShare

http://www.beyond-software.com/Software/Webshare.html .3
   Web server for IBM/VM/CMS.

VAX/VMS

Gopher Software Distribution for VAX/VMS

ftp://boombox.micro.umn.edu:/pub/gopher
gopher://boombox.micro.umn.edu/1/gopher
   Gopher server and client software for VAX/VMS platforms.

Listserv (L-Soft Listserv)

http://www.lsoft.com
ftp://ftp.lsoft.com
gopher://gopher.lsoft.com
(Send e-mail to lsv-info@bitnic.educom.org.)
   The L-Soft Listserv, or Revised Listserv, is the original Listserv software written by Eric Thomas. It is available for Unix, IBM/VM/CMS, VAX/VMS, and Windows NT.

Mailserv Software

A guide for Mailserv can be retrieved by sending e-mail to mailserv@ac.dal.ca (or other Mailserv address) with the message help.
   Mailserv is VAX/VMS–based e-mail distribution management software for discussion lists and electronic journal. It does not, how-

ever, have automated discussion list archiving, and does not have file archive searching capabilities. Mailserv is included with the widely used PMDF mail agent software package, available from Innosoft International, Inc., of Claremont, California.

MS WINDOWS PCs (INCLUDING WINDOWS 95, WINDOWS NT, WINDOWS 3.1, AND WINDOWS FOR WORKGROUPS

Alibaba
http://www.csm.co.at/csm/
   Windows Web server by CSM.

BBN Internet Server and Frontdoor v1.2
http://www.bbn.com
   Windows Web server by CSM.

CL-HTTP: Common Lisp Hypermedia Server
http://www.ai.mit.edu/projects/iiip/doc/cl-http/home-page.html
   Web server software by John C. Mallery for Macintosh and Windows.

Consensys InterWare
http://www.consensys.com
   The "First Complete Family of Internet Servers for Windows NT." Commercial site offering Windows NT Internet server software and instructions. "InterWare is a highly integrated family of software components that provide everything you need to set up a professional Internet server on a computer running Windows NT. InterWare comes with a comprehensive and easy to use interface for administering each Internet server along with a number of examples of server-based applications."

Consummate Windows Applications Collection
http://www.charm.net/CWSApps/
   Our second-favorite site!

GIF and JPEG Viewing Software for Windows (LVIEW and WINJPEG)
ftp://ftp.ftp.com/support/pub/windows

Gopher Server for Windows NT

ftp://emwac.ed.ac.uk/pub/gophers/

Gopher server based on the Microsoft Windows NT operating system written by Chris Adie.

Gopher Software Distribution for Windows, Windows NT, Windows 95, etc.

ftp://boombox.micro.umn.edu:/pub/gopher
gopher://boombox.micro.umn.edu/1/gopher

Gopher server and client software for all current versions of Windows.

Listserv (LSOFT Listserv)

http://www.lsoft.com
ftp://ftp.lsoft.com
gopher://gopher.lsoft.com
(Send e-mail to lsv-info@bitnic.educom.org.)

The L-Soft Listserv, or Revised Listserv, is the original Listserv software written by Eric Thomas. It is available for Unix, IBM/VM/CMS, VAX/VMS, and Windows NT.

NCSA HTTPd

http://hoohoo.ncsa.uiuc.edu/
ftp://ftp.ncsa.uiuc.edu/Web

The HTTPd Web server software for Windows, Windows NT, and Unix.

NetMagic WebServer (TM)

http://www.aristosoft.com/netmagic/company.html

Web server for Windows NT and Windows 95. Includes Web chatroom software that enables organizations to host live help desks and discussion groups.

NovaServer 4

http://www.resnova.com/product/

Web server software (for 4D database system) by ResNova for Macintosh and Windows.

NTMAIL

http://www.net-shopper.co.uk/software/ntmail/index.htm

SMTP and POP3 server capabilities for Windows NT. It will also work as a Listserv.

Polyform
ftp://ftp.portal.com/pub/cbntmkr/polyform.zip

CGI forms handling package, written by Mark Bracewell, that can create forms for customer feedback, provide automatic mail response to customers, and a variety of other applications. It is easy to configure and requires no programming to use. It is implemented for the WHTTPd server.

Purveyor WebServer
http://www.process.com/

Windows Web server by Process Software Corp.

SERV-U
ftp://oak.oakland.edu/SimTel/win3/winsock

FTP server written by Rob Beckers for Microsoft Windows 3.1.

SerWeb
ftp://sunsite.unc.edu/pub/micro/pc-stuff/ms-windows/winsock/apps

Freeware Web server written in C++ by Gustavo Estrella for Microsoft 3.1 or Windows NT.

TCP/IP and Related Software
ftp://ftp.ncsa.uiuc.edu
ftp://ftp.utas.edu.au
gopher://ici.proper.com
(Pick the directory for your type of computer.)

TCP/IP–related software for Macintosh, DOS, Windows, and Unix. Includes WWW clients and servers, Winsock applications, NCSA telnet, graphics viewing software, sound applications, and WAIS and Archie clients software.

TeleFinder BBS
http://www.spiderisland.com/

Web server software by Spider Island Software for Macintosh and Windows

Trumpet Winsock
ftp://ftp.utas.edu.au/pc/trumpet/winsock/

Winsock-compliant TCP/IP software written by Peter Tattam. Required to run any Winsock-compliant Internet servers on the Windows platform.

The Ultimate Collection of Winsock Software!
http://gfn1.genesee.freenet.org/tucows/
   "The world's best collection of Winsock Software, Tools and Utilities on the 'Net!"

Web4HAM
ftp://ftp.informatik.uni-hamburg.de/pub/net/winsock
   Web server, developed by Gunter Hille at the University of Hamburg, for Windows.

Web Server for Windows NT
ftp://emwac.ed.ac.uk/pub/https/
   Web server written by Chris Adie for Windows NT.

WebSTAR 95/NT
http://www.quarterdeck.com/
   Windows 95 and Windows NT Web server.

WebSite
http://software.ora.com/download/
   Web server for Windows 95 and Windows NT written by Bob Denny in cooperation with O'Reilly & Associates. This is one of our favorites.

WFTPd FTP Server
ftp://sunsite.unc.edu/pub/micro/pc-stuff/ms-windows/winsock/apps/
   FTP server written by Alun Jones for Windows 3.1.

WHTTPd
http://www.city.net/win-httpd
   Web server written by Bob Denny for Windows. The functionality is similar to the Unix Web server HTTPd.

Windows NT FTP Server
http://www.microsoft.com
   Windows NT comes with an FTP server. Check Microsoft's Web server for more information.

Windows SMTP Mail Server
ftp://sunsite.unc.edu/pub/micro/pc-stuff/ms-windows/winsock/apps

WinQVT/Net

ftp://biochemistry.bioc.cwru.edu/gopher/pub/winqvt

TCP/IP client and server applications for the Windows environment provided by QPC Software as a shareware product. Includes telnet and FTP clients as well as an FTP server.

Winsock (TCP/IP Standard for Windows)

ftp://ftp.ftp.com/support/pub/winsock
gopher://ici.proper.com

These sites contain Winsock-compliant TCP/IP shareware for Windows. Also other Winsock compatible Internet tools (such as WS_FTP) are available at this site.

ZBServer

http://www.zbserver.com/

Web and Gopher server in one, written by Bob Bradley, for Windows 3.1 and Windows 95.

Appendix B

Directory of Selected Tutorials and FAQs on Setting Up Internet Service and Client Software

Note: These are tutorials available through the Internet on how to set up Internet servers or build Internet applications. Some of these tutorials are accompanied by the distribution of the software. These tutorials are written for individuals with advanced Internet knowledge. The information on setting up servers on Macintoshes and some other microcomputer systems are fairly simple, but some of these tutorials are written for individuals with significant computer systems administration experience to set up the software on a particular platform.

Accessing a Database Server via the World Wide Web
http://cscsun1.larc.nasa.gov/~beowulf/db/

Collection of reviews, tutorials, and source sites for free, shareware, and commercial Web/database gateway software for all platforms. Maintained by J. P. Rowe (j.p.rowe@larc.nasa.gov).

Beginner's Guide to URLs
http://www.ncsa.uiuc.edu/demoweb/url-primer.html

Necessary information about Uniform Resource Locators.

Building Web Servers
http://www.cybergroup.com

This site is maintained by Cybergroup Inc., a World Wide Web training and consulting firm. It is a clear, simple discussion of Web server choices and computer platform choices. This site also has links to tutorials and software for FTP, telnet, and Gopher servers and clients. Cybergroup also provides its own basic tutorials that are excellent for the beginning Internet information producer and provider. One of their tutorials deals with finding a Web server through commercial Internet providers. This would be an excellent option for a library that did not want or could not afford to set up its own server locally.

CGI: Common Gateway Interface Tutorial
http://hoohoo.ncsa.uiuc.edu/cgi/

Excellent tutorial on CGI bin scripting. CGI bin scripts can be written in any computer language that can be run on your system (for example, Perl, C, C++, Applescript, Visual Basic, and Unix shell scripts). Explains installation of CGI scripts in the /cgi-bin directory under the NCSA HTTPd Web servers.

The CyberWebs
http://www.charm.net/~web

Site with many tutorials on topics such as CGI, HTML, and Web server installation.

Description of Internet Services
ftp://ftp.shell.portal.com/pub/chan/services.html

Overview of Internet services software. What they do and what they can be used for. Written by Jeff Chan (chan@shell.portal.com).

Discussion Lists: Mail List Manager Commands
http://lawlib.slu.edu/training/mailser.htm

Tutorial on Listserv, Listproc, and Majordomo management, written by James Milles. This is a must-read for anyone intending to use any of these programs to distribute an e-journal or e-newsletter.

Entering the World Wide Web: A Guide to Cyberspace
http://epics.aps.anl.gov/demo/guide/www.guide.html

Kevin Hughes provides a good overview of the Web, including general Web information and how to obtain Web browsers and servers.

FAQ's on Just about Everything

http://www.cis.ohio-state.edu/hypertext/faq/usenet/top.html
    Many FAQs from Usenet newsgroups on multiple topics.

Gopher FAQ

gopher://mudhoney.micro.umn.edu/00/Gopher.FAQ
    Frequently asked questions about Gopher, including how to set up Gopher servers and clients, and where to retrieve them.

HTML Language Manual

http://www.utirc.utoronto.ca/HTMLdocs/NewHTML/intro.html
    This manual is written by Ian Graham and includes treatises on ISINDEX, FORMS, ISMAP, CGI-bin scripts/programs, and other useful features.

An Information Provider's Guide to Web Servers

http://www.vuw.ac.nz/non-local/gnat/www-servers.html
    Overview of selected World Wide Web server software.

Java Self Study Tutorial

http://www.tegosoft.Inter.net/tegojava.html#Start
    Courtesy of TegoSoft this tutorial includes free Java Applets and instructions for creating a Web page that includes Java Applets. The tutorial is in PDF format and requires the Adobe Acrobat Reader to use.

Java Workshop (Thingtone's Java Workshop)

http://users.aol.com/thingtone/workshop/index.htm
    Tutorial prepared by Russ Ethington (Russ.Eth@ix.netcom.com). It is a detailed Java programming workshop for the experienced programmer.

Linux Documentation Project

http://amelia.experiment.db.erau.edu/ldp/linux.html
    Linux is a complete, copylefted (copyright statement that says the product is freely available and that all derivative works must also be freely available), Unix clone for Intel 386/486/Pentium machines. It includes emacs, X11R6, gcc, TeX/LaTeX, groff, TCP/IP, SLIP, UUCP, the works. This site has everything you ever wanted to know about Linux but were afraid to ask. (Description taken from the page.)

Listproc (Cren's Listprocessor)

http://www.cren.net/listproc/

Listproc central information site has product information, licensing, and instructions.

Listserv (L-Soft Listserv)

http://www.lsoft.com

L-Soft's central clearinghouse for the Listserv software has product information, tutorials and FAQs as well as installation and management instructions.

Majordomo FAQ and Other Tutorials

ftp://ftp.greatcircle.com/pub/majordomo/
http://www.greatcircle.com/majordomo/

Just about everything you want to know about Majordomo.

MIME FAQ

http://www.cis.ohio-state.edu/hypertext/faq/usenet/mail/mime-faq/top.html

Everything you want to know about the MIME (Multipurpose Internet Mail Extensions) standard and its implementation.

NCSA HTTPd Tutorial

http://hoohoo.ncsa.uiuc.edu/docs/tutorials/

Detailed instructions for installation, security, and even CGI scripting.

Novell's World Wide Web Homepage

http://www.novell.com

Access to documentation and information about Novell NetWare and new products. Includes much information about TCP/IP networking over existing Novell NetWare LANs.

PC-Mac TCP/IP and NFS FAQ List

http://www.rtd.com/pcnfsfaq/faq.html

This frequently-asked-questions file is written by Rawn Shah. He answers many TCP/IP questions for the PC and Macintosh and provides links to helpful networking software.

PDIAL: Public Dialup Internet Access List

http://WWW.pdial.com
ftp://ftp.best.com:/pub/kaminski

(Send e-mail to info-deli-server@pdial.com with the message SEND PDIAL.)

Directory of public or commerical Internet access service providers.

Personal IP
http://www.charm.net/ppp.html

Tutorial written Craig Nordin of Charm Net provides overview and helpful links on how to work with SLIP, PPP, and Winsock.

Registering your Web Server with the World Wide Web Consortium
http://www.w3.org/hypertext/DataSources/WWW/Geographical_generation/new-servers.html

All you'll need to do is connect to the URL above and fill in their form.

Tutorial on Setting Up a Server on a Microcomputer
http://130.85.10.39/slide01.htm

General overview of the software available and how to set it up.

Usenet "How to Become a USENET Site"
ftp://rtfm.mit.edu/pub/usenet/news.announce.newuser

Details the procedures for retrieving the Usenet newsgroup software, and the basics of setting it up.

The Web Developer's Virtual Library
http://www.stars.com

The best of the many Web developer resource centers. Includes tutorials and links to other tutorials on HTML, CGI, Images, Perl, and much more.

Web FAQ
http://siva.cshl.org/~boutell/www_faq.html

Frequently asked questions about the World Wide Web, including how to set up Web servers and where to retrieve them.

WebCompare Web Browser Features Comparison
http://www.webcompare.com/browser-main.html

Overview of Web client software with reviews and basic functionalities.

WebCompare Web Servers Comparisons
http://www.proper.com/www/servers-chart.html
   Overview of Web server software with reviews and basic functionalities.

World Wide Web Client Software Meta Resource List
http://www.comvista.com/us/lea/servers.html
   Attempt to create a comprehensive list of available Web client software. Compiled by Lea Silk (lsilk@comvista.com).

World Wide Web Security FAQ
http://www-genome.wi.mit.edu/WWW/faqs/www-security-faq.html
   Very comprehensive discussion of Web security: what to worry about, how to prevent problems, and how to run a Web server from behind a Firewall, plus lots more. Maintained by Lincoln D. Stein (lstein@genome.wi.mit.edu).

World Wide Web Server Software Meta Resource List
http://www.comvista.com/us/lea/servers.html
   Attempt to create a comprehensive list of available Web server software. Compiled by Lea Silk (lsilk@comvista.com).

World Wide Web Tools for Aspiring Web Weavers
http://www.nas.nasa.gov/RNR/Education/geninfo.html
   Resource center for the Web developer. Many useful tools are available here.

WWW and HTML Developer's JumpStation
http://oneworld.wa.com/htmldev/devpage/dev
   Lots of information about the World Wide Web.

Appendix C

Just Enough Unix

TABLE OF CONTENTS

INTRODUCTION TO UNIX

Note: The convention used in these training materials is to print in boldface commands or text words to be typed. Variables that would require typing in actual data such as *filename, directoryname, –options list* are italicized.

Unix History and Evolution

Unix is a multiuser, multitasking operating system that is available for most hardware platforms regardless of brand name. The Unix operating system includes programs that allow editing files, running programs, sending and receiving e-mail, and many other functions.

Unix was invented by Ken Thompson, a researcher at AT&T Bell Labs in the late 1960s. It was first made available as a commercial product in 1970. Since then Unix has been developed further both by the academic community and commercially (specifically the University of California at Berkeley's Computer Science Research Group's BSD Unix, which has been distributed freely on the Internet for most mini- and microcomputers). Commercial development continued concurrently with the academic development, and versions of Unix specific to proprietary computer hardware platforms have been developed. For example AIX is Unix for IBM, HP-UX is for Hewlett-Packard, and Ultrix is for Digital Equipment Corporation (DEC) minicomputers and workstations. In 1992 AT&T sold its Unix operations to Novell and BSD Unix was licensed by Berkeley Software Development, Inc.

Unix Terminology

PID:
　Process ID. The process ID is useful for **fg** or killing a process.

Shell:
　The shell is the user interface with the Unix operating system. There are three major shells in general use: Korn, Bourne, and C. Korn and Bourne are the most commonly used shells. The default shell prompt for the Bourne and Korn shells is "$" while the C shell uses "%" (the Korn and C shell prompts can be changed, much like

the DOS prompt). Most Unix commands are typed at the shell prompt. If your system starts up with a menu, pressing ctrl-C to escape from the menu to get to the shell prompt might work.

Moving Through and Displaying Directories

List files in a directory:

ls *-options list*
This command is comparable to *dir* in DOS. The options available are:

-a
Displays all the files and subdirectories in the current directory including the parent directory and system directories to which your account is pointed for running the shell and other programs from the system.

-l
Displays information about each file and subdirectory. Includes

- information about the total number of files in the current directory
- whether it is a directory or a plain file (d is directory, - is file)
- access modes (owner, group, and others)
- who created or owns the file (userid or group name)
- the size of the file in bytes
- when it was last modified
- the name of the file or directory

* ? [](wildcards)
You can also list files that contain some characters in common, e.g., **ls *.txt** will list all files that end with .txt.

The **?** stands in for any single letter. So **ls wom?n** will find all files that begin wom, any other single letter, and end with n.

[] will surround any choice of characters that you might use. This is useful when you aren't sure what case the letters might be or when you want to get all possible cases such as **ls [Tt]emp.**

Print Working Directory

pwd
This command displays the name of your current directory to the screen.

The following commands in Unix are similar to those used in DOS; however in Unix these commands are case sensitive. So, if you want to change directory to TEMP, you must type **TEMP** in all upper case. If the directory is called MyStuff, you must type the *directoryname* in mixed case exactly as it is named. As in DOS you can change directories through subdirectory nesting, e.g., **cd TEMP/subtemp** will change the current directory to subtemp. Note that Unix uses the forward slash (/) and DOS uses the back slash (\).

Return to Home Directory

cd

Change to a New Directory

cd *path/directoryname*

Move Up a Directory

cd ..

Check Disk Quota Used

quota -v

Creating New Directories

mkdir *path/directoryname*
This command should be very familiar to anyone who has used DOS. It performs the same function—creating new directories or subdirectories—in Unix.

Deleting (Removing) Empty Directories

rmdir *path/directoryname*
As in DOS the **rmdir** command requires that the directory be
empty before it can be deleted.

Looking at and in Files

Display file contents (continuous):
cat *filename*(s)

Display file contents a screen at a time:
more *filename*
These commands are similar to the **type** command in DOS. The
continuous **cat** will quit displaying when the entire file has been
displayed. It is best used with shorter files. If you type **cat** without a *filename*, press ctrl-D to stop it.

The **more** command displays a file one page at a time. You
can move around in the file but it is read-only. Following are
commands to move around in **more**:

- next page: space bar
- move down one line: enter
- move forward multiple pages: **nf** (where n is the number
  of pages)
- move backward one or more pages: **b** or **nb**
- find a word forward in the file: **/word**
- find a word backward in the file: **?word**
- redisplay a page: ctrl-L
- review options/get help: **h**
- edit the file: **v**
- quit more: **q**

Setting File Access Privileges

chmod *-permissions filename*
chmod *-permissions directoryname*
The chmod command is used to change the mode of access to a
file or directory. Only the owner of a file or directory is allowed
to change the mode of access. Use **ls -l** to find out who owns a
file or directory. For example, **chmod a+r** allows all people with

access to the system to read the file or enter a directory, but not to delete, rename, or change the file.

Copying, Moving, and Renaming Files or Directories

Copy a file:
cp oldpath/*filename*/newpath/*filename*

Moving or renaming a file or directory:
mv oldpath/*filename* newpath/*filename*
mv oldpath/*directoryname* new path/*directoryname*

The **cp** command copies the contents of a file to a new file and/or subdirectory. The original file continues to exist in its original location. The **mv** command moves the file to a new file and/or subdirectory; the original *filename* is discontinued.

Creating, Changing, and Deleting Files

Creating a new file:
(general syntax: editing program name new *filename*)
emacs *newfilename*
pico *newfilename*

Editing an existing file:
emacs *filename*
pico *filename*

Deleting files:
rm oldpath/*filename* newpath/*filename*

The emacs program is a Unix text editor. It has commands that allow movement within a file, editing the contents of a file and saving a file. It can be used to create a new file or to edit an existing file. Following are emacs commands:

- delete current line: ctrl-k
- save (write) and quit: ctrl-x ctrl-c
- save (write): ctrl-x **s**

Starting and Stopping Processes

Running programs (processes):
Generally type the program name at the shell prompt

Stop a running process at the shell prompt:
kill PID

Interrupt a process from within:
ctrl-c

General Useful Commands

compress files:	**compress** bigfile
change your password:	**passwd**
consult on-line manuals:	**man** commandname
list your processes and their PIDs	**ps**
list other users currently logged in:	**who**, **w,** or **finger**

Appendix D

Directory of Discussion Lists and Newsgroups for Internet Information Producers or Providers (IIPOPs)

ADV-CGI
Contact: Adam Donahue adam.donahue@nyu.edu
ADV-CGI is a heavily moderated discussion list provided by the Academic Computing at New York University. The ADV-CGI list is for the discussion of all applications of the Common Gateway Interface. Other advanced Web programming topics may also be discussed.

> Send e-mail to listproc@lists.nyu.edu with the message: subscribe adv-cgi Yourfirstname Yourlastname

ADV-HTML
Contact: Patrick Douglas Crispen PCRISPE1@ua1vm.ua.edu
Discussion of the latest and most complex Hypertext Markup Language (HTML) tags. This list is designed for experienced Webmasters, SysOps, Internet Trainers, and advanced Web page authors. Since ADV-HTML is an *advanced* list, it is assumed that the ADV-HTML subscribers already have extensive knowledge of, and experience with, basic HTML tags. If you do not already know how to create your own World Wide Web homepage using Hypertext Markup Language, it is strongly recommended that you

NOT subscribe to ADV-HTML (instead, you should point your World Wide Web browser to the "Beginner's Guide to HTML" at http://www.ncsa.uiuc.edu/General/Internet/WWW/HTMLPrimer.html).

Send e-mail to listserv@ua1vm.ua.edu with the message subscribe adv-html Yourfirstname Yourlastname

alt.security.pgp

Discussion of PGP (Pretty Good Privacy) technical and political issues. PGP-PUBLIC-KEYS on majordomo@c2.org is a group where public keys are distributed

Use a Usenet Newsreader to connect to alt.security.pgp

BESTWEB

Contact: Veli HAZAR sysadm8@vm.ege.edu.tr

Discussion of the best web sites world-wide

Send email to listserv@vm.ege.edu.tr with the message: subscribe bestweb Yourfirstname Yourlastname

BUSLIB-L

Contact: Barbara Butler butler@equinox.unr.edu

Discussion forum for issues related to business libraries.

Send email to listserv@idbsu.idbsu.edu with the message: sub-scribe buslib-l Yourfirstname Yourlastname or use a Usenet Newsreader to connect to bit.listserv.buslib-l

C-EDRES

Contact: Lynn Thomas d616@unb.ca

Forum to announce, describe, and evaluate educational resources available on the Internet. Its companion list, EDRES-DB, func-tions as a database for these resources.

Send e-mail to c-edres-server@unb.ca

Archives: http://www.cua.edu — gopher://vmsgopher.cua.edu.:70/11gopher_root_eric_ae:[_edres] - gopher gopher.cua.edu

Cisco

Contact: David Wood cisco-request@spot.Colorado.EDU

Discussion of the network products from Cisco Systems, Inc; pri-marily their gateway products, but also their terminal servers, pro-tocol converters, FDDI concentrators, ATM switches, and any other relevant products. Discussions about operation, problems, features, topology, configuration, protocols, routing, loading, serving, etc are all encouraged. Other topics include vendor relations, new product announcements, availability of fixes and new features, and discusion of new requirements and desirable features. This mailing list also feeds the comp.dcom.sys.cisco usenet news group. At this time, articles posted to the newsgroup are not forwarded to the mailing list.

Send e-mail to cisco-request@spot.Colorado.EDU

Archives: http://www.cisco.com/ — ftp://spot.Colorado.EDU/cisco

CNI-COPYRIGHT

Contact: Mary Brandt Jensen CNICOPY@CHARLIE.USD.EDU—Czeslaw Jan Grycz CJG@STUBBS.UCOP.EDU—Craig A. Summerhill CRAIG@cni.org

CNI Copyright and Intellectual Property Forum. Sponsored by the Coalition for Networked Information.

Send e-mail to listproc@cni.org with the message subscribe cni-copyright Yourfirstname Yourlastname

CNI-DIRECTORIES

Contact: George Brett GHB@CONCERT.NET—Peggy Seiden PSEIDEN@SKIDMORE.EDU—Craig A. Summerhill CRAIG@cni.org

CNI Directories and Information Resource Services Working Group. This is the official forum of the Coalition for Networked Information's Directories and Resource Information Services Working Group. The discussion is related to the development of directory and information resource services in networked environments and related topics. Sponsored by the Coalition for Networked Information.

Send e-mail to listproc@cni.org with the message subscribe cni-directories Yourfirstname Yourlastname

CNI-LEGISLATION

Contact: Peter S. Graham Graham@ZODIAC.RUTGERS.EDU—Craig A. Summerhill CRAIG@cni.org

CNI Legislation, Policies, Codes and Practices Working Group. Sponsored by the Coalition for Networked Information.

Send e-mail to listproc@cni.org with the message subscribe cni-legislation Yourfirstname Yourlastname

CNI-MODERNIZATION
Contact: Dorothy Gregor
DGREGOR@LIBRARY. BERKELEY.EDU— Karen Hunter
KHUNTER@pucc.princeton.edu—Craig A. Summerhill
CRAIG@cni.org
CNI Modernization of Scholarly Publication Working Group. Sponsored by the Coalition for Networked Information.

Send e-mail to listproc@cni.org with the message subscribe cni-modernization Yourfirstname Yourlastname

CNI-PUBINFO
Contact: Barbara von Wahlde UNLBVW@ubvm.cc.buffalo.edu—
John L. Hankins HANKINS@CIC.NET—Craig A. Summerhill
CRAIG@cni.org
CNI Access to Public Information Working Group. Sponsored by the Coalition for Networked Information.

Send e-mail to listproc@cni.org with the message subscribe cni-pubinfo Yourfirstname Yourlastname

CNI-TRANSFORMATION
Contact: Charles Henry CHHENRY@VASSAR.EDU—Peter
Lyman LYMAN@VM.USC.EDU—Craig A. Summerhill
CRAIG@cni.org
CNI Transformation of Scholarly Communication Working Group. Sponsored by the Coalition for Networked Information.

Send e-mail to listproc@cni.org with the message subscribe cni-transformation Yourfirstname Yourlastname

COM-PRIV
Contact: listadm@lists.psi.com
An e-conference devoted to discussing the commercialization of the Internet.

Send e-mail to listproc@lists.psi.com
Archives: ftp://com-priv uu.psi.com//archive/com-priv/

comp.archives
Contact: Edward Vielmetti comp-archives@msen.com
Descriptions of public access software archives and new additions to them.

Use a Usenet Newsreader to connect to comp.archives
Archives: ftp://rtfm.mit.edu/comp.archives/

comp.archives.admin
Contact: Edward Vielmetti comp-archives@msen.com
Discussion of issues relating to computer archive administration.
   Use a Usenet Newsreader to connect to comp.archives.admin
   Archives: ftp://rtfm.mit.edu/comp.archives.admin/

comp.archives.msdos.*
Contact: Keith Petersen, Timo Salmi, Ari Hovila and Brian O'Neill msdos-ann-request@SimTel.Coast.NET
comp.archives.msdos.announce: Announcements about MS-DOS and Microsoft Windows public software archives. (Moderated) - comp.archives.msdos.d: Discussion of materials available in MS-DOS and Microsoft Windows archives.
   Use a Usenet Newsreader to connect to comp.archives.msdos.*
   Archives: ftp://rtfm.mit.edu/comp.archives.msdos.announce/
   ftp://rtfm.mit.edu/comp.archives.msdos.d/

comp.security.*
Discussions about computer security issues.—comp.security. announce: announcements from the NSF's Computer Emergency Response Team (Moderated by cert@cert.org, archived at cert.org in the directory pub/cert_advisories); not for discussion.—comp.security.misc: Discussion of all computer and network security issues.—comp.security.unix: Discussion of Unix security.
   Send e-mail to Local Usenet Newsreader
   Archives: ftp://rtfm.mit.edu/comp.security.misc/ —
   ftp://rtfm.mit.edu/comp.security.unix/

CPSR-ANNOUNCE
Contact: Paul Hyland phyland@gwuvm.edu
CPSR-ANNOUNCE is an e-conference for CPSR-related materials and announcements. Sponsored by Computer Professionals for Social Responsibility.
   Send e-mail to listserv@cpsr.org with the message subscribe cpsr-announce Yourfirstname Yourlastname

CYBERIA-L
Computer network policy and the Law
   Send e-mail to listserv@listserv.CC.WM.EDU with the message subscribe cyberia-l Yourfirstname Yourlastname

DIGLIB

Contact Address: Terry Kuny ifla@nlc-bnc.ca

DIGLIB is an Internet mailing list for librarians, information scientists, and other information professionals to discuss the constellation of issues and technologies pertaining to the creation of digital libraries.

> Send e-mail to listserv@infoserv.nlc-bnc.ca with the message subscribe diglib Yourfirstname Yourlastname

FIREWALLS

Contact: Michael C. Berch mcb@greatcircle.com

The Firewalls mailing list is for discussions of the design, construction, maintenance, and management of Internet security firewall systems. An Internet security firewall system might be defined as any system that lets a site take advantage of the services offered by the Internet, while protecting that site against attack from the Internet. FIREWALLS-DIGEST and FIREWALLS-STANDARDS are also available.

> Send e-mail to majordomo@GREATCIRCLE.COM with the message subscribe firewalls youremailaddress
> Archives: ftp://ftp.GreatCircle.COM/pub/firewalls/archives.

GOVPUB

Contact: Dana Noonan noonan@msus1.msus.edu

Devoted to the practical and policy issues related to providing local and state government information on the Internet. It is not a forum for political debate. This list is intended for agency professional and technical staff involved in making public information available online, but anyone with an interest in the topic is welcome to join the list.

> Send e-mail to listserv@listserv.nodak.edu with the message subscribe govpub Yourfirstname Yourlastname

HTML-L

Contact: Turgut Kalfaoglu turgut@vm.ege.edu.tr

The HTML-L list is for assistance with questions on the creation of WWW (World Wide Web) pages, including CGI scripts, home pages, etc.

> Send e-mail to listserv@vm.ege.edu.tr with the message: subscribe html-l Yourfirstname Yourlastname

HYTELNET

Contact Address: Peter Scott aa375@freenet.carleton.ca
This list is for announcements of new versions of the popular HYTELNET program, which gives a user access to all known telnet-accessible sites on the Internet. List members will also receive announcements of new/changed/defunct sites, announced between full versions of the program.

Send e-mail to listserv@library.berkeley.edu with the message subscribe hytelnet Yourfirstname Yourlastname

INETBIB

Contact Address: Michael Schaarwaechter
michael.schaarwaechter@zb.ub.uni-dortmund.de
Discussion of Internet usage in German or German-speaking libraries. English language messages are accepted.

Send e-mail to maiser@zb.ub.uni-dortmund.de with the message subscribe inetbib Yourfirstname Yourlastname
Archives: http://www.ub.uni-dortmund.de

INTERNET-MARKETING

Contact: Glenn Fleishman glenn@popco.com
The topic of marketing and Internet is a broad one and controversial. This list was established to discuss *appropriate* marketing of services, ideas, and items to and on the Internet. At this writing, over 1,000 people and sites involved in all aspects of marketing, sales, programming, journalism, and other fields are actively participating in this forum.

Send e-mail to listproc@popco.com with the message subscribe internet-marketing Yourfirstname Yourlastname
Archives: http://www.popco.com/hyper/inet-marketing

ISDN

Contact: Per Sigmond isdn-request@dumbcat.sf.ca.us
ISDN is open for discussion of all aspects specific to ISDN (protocols, services, applications, experiences, status, coverage, implementations, etc.)

Send e-mail to majordomo@dumbcat.sf.ca.us with the message subscribe ISDN youremailaddress
Archives: ftp://ugle.unit.no/archives

JAVA-MAC

Contact: Sandy Schneible java-mac-owner@natural.com or sandra@natural.com

Discusses software development using Sun Microsystem's Java language on the Apple Macintosh computer. Topics may range from discussion of tools, techniques, solutions, tech notes, and any other items of relevant interest to Macintosh Java developers.

> Send e-mail to majordomo@natural.com with the message subscribe java-mac Yourfirstname Yourlastname

LIBREF-L

Contact: LIBREF-L Moderators librefed@kentvm.kent.edu — Kara L. Robinson krobinso@kentvm.kent.edu

LIBREF-L was created in response to a perceived desire for a quick and interactive communications medium for reference librarians. This is a discussion of the changing environment of library reference services and activities.

> Send email to listserv@kentvm.kent.edu with the message: subscribe libref-l Yourfirstname Yourlastname or use a Usenet Newsreader to connect to bit.listserv.libref-l

List-Managers

Contact: Michael C. Berch mcb@GreatCircle.COM

A discussion group for managers (moderators, owners, etc.) of electronic mailing lists. Topics include (but are not limited to) list management software, policy issues, list management techniques, and troubleshooting. There is a digest version of the list available as List-Managers-Digest@GreatCircle.COM.

> Send e-mail to majordomo@GreatCircle.COM with the message subscribe list-managers Youremailaddress
> Archives: ftp://ftp.greatcircle.com/pub/list-managers/archive.

LM_NET

Contact: Peter Milbury pmilbur@eis.calstate.edu

School Library Media e-conference that focuses on the topics of interest to the school library media community, including the latest on school library media services, operations, and activities. It is an e-conference of practitioners helping practitioners . . . linking schools through their library media centers.

> Send email to lm_net-request@listserv.syr.edu with the message: subscribe lm_net Yourfirstname Yourlastname

LSTOWN-L
Contact: Eric Thomas ERIC@searn.sunet.se
Forum for list owners of mailing lists managed by L-Soft International's listserv product (VM, VMS, unix). Eric Thomas (eric@searn.sunet.se) is the author of the original listserv software (written in 1986 for VM systems).

Send e-mail to listserv@searn.sunet.se with the message subscribe lstown-l Yourfirstname Yourlastname

LSTSRV-L
Contact: Eric Thomas ERIC@searn.sunet.se
Forum for owners/operators of the L-Soft international's listserv software written by Eric Thomas (ERIC@SEARN).

Send e-mail to listserv@searn.sunet.se with the message subscribe lstsrv-l Yourfirstname Yourlastname

Majordomo-Announce
Contact: Michael C. Berch mcb@GreatCircle.COM
For announcements of new releases of the Majordomo mailing list manager.

Send e-mail to majordomo@GreatCircle.COM with the message subscribe majordomo-announce Youremailaddress
Archives: Yes. ftp://ftp.greatcircle.com/pub/list-managers/archive

Majordomo-Users
Contact: Michael C. Berch mcb@GreatCircle.COM
A discussion group for users of Majordomo electronic mailing list servers.

Send e-mail to majordomo@GreatCircle.COM with the message subscribe majordomo-users Youremailaddress
Archives: Yes. ftp://ftp.greatcircle.com/pub/

Majordomo-Workers
Contact: Michael C. Berch mcb@GreatCircle.COM
A discussion group for managers (moderators, owners, etc.) of Majordomo electronic mailing list servers.

Send e-mail to majordomo@GreatCircle.COM with the message subscribe majordomo-workers Youremailaddress
Archives: Yes. ftp://ftp.greatcircle.com/pub/

MEDIAWEB
Contact: Jim Loter jloter@blue.weeg.uiowa.edu

MEDIAWEB is a loose coalition of film/TV/video webmasters that seeks to foster collaboration and to minimize the redundancy of materials on film/TV/video WWW sites. MediaWeb is open to all, but it is not really intended for the users of these sites. Rather, it aims to assist film/TV/video webmasters so that they might better coordinate their efforts.

> Send e-mail to listserv@vm.temple.edu with the message subscribe mediaweb Yourfirstname Yourlastname

MEDLIB-L
Contact: Nancy Start hslstart@ubvm.cc.buffalo.edu

MEDLIB-L is an e-conference for medical and health sciences libraries. Practical and theoretical issues in public and technical services are discussed. This forum is for ideas, questions, announcements, and concerns specific to health sciences libraries. Sponsored by the Medical Library Association.

> Send email to listserv@listserv.acsu.buffalo.edu with the message: subscribe libref-l Yourfirstname Yourlastname or use a Usenet Newsreader to connect to bit.listserv.medlib-l

MVSGOPHER
Contact: Duane Weaver weaver@ohstmvsa.acs.ohio-state.edu

Discussion of the MVS implementation of the Gopher client and server.

> Send e-mail to listserver@lists.acs.ohio-state.edu with the message subscribe mvsgopher Yourfirstname Yourlastname

NativeWeb
Contact: Al Mandell almandel@sfsu.edu —
mandell@bioc02.uthscsa.edu

A forum that will discuss issues regarding Indigenous Peoples' resources on the World Wide Web. Suggestions and help to people who are creating their own web pages.

> Send e-mail to listserv@thecity.sfsu.edu with the message subscribe nativeweb Yourfirstname Yourlastname

NET-HAPPENINGS/NET-RESOURCES
Contact: Gleason Sackman

Announcements of new Internet Resources and excerpts from various discussions of Internet related events. Sub-topics include net-sites, net-zines, net-events, net-misc. Read the new-user message for directions on how to set sub-topics. net-happenings-digest is also available.

> Send e-mail to majordomo@dsmail.internic.net with the message subscribe net-happenings Youremailaddress or use a Usenet Newsreader to connect to comp.internet.net-happenings
> Archives: http://www.mid.net/net/

NETTRAIN

Contact: Jim Milles MILLESJG@SLUVCA.SLU.EDU

E-conference for librarians, computer support personnel, computer jocks—all those who are involved in teaching others how to use the Internet. Topics for discussion include such areas as: how to divide responsibility for teaching internetwork use; methods of teaching and resources used; and policies on access (faculty, student, staff) to the networks. NETTRAIN is, therefore, intended for experienced users of Internet, *not* for beginners looking for help with basic questions.

> Send e-mail to listserv@listserv.acsu.buffalo.edu with the message subscribe nettrain Yourfirstname Yourlastname or Use a Usenet Newsreader to connect to bit.listserv.nettrain

NEW-LIST

Contact: Marty Hoag HOAG@plains.nodak.edu

A central address to post announcements of new public mailing lists. In addition, "NEW-LIST" might be used as a final verification before establishing an list (to check for existing lists on the same topic, etc.). However, be sure to check sources such as the Internet List-of-Lists (SIGLIST or INTEREST-GROUPS list), listserv GROUPS, Usenet News newusers lists, and the LISTS database on the major listservs (we have the LISTS database on vm1.nodak.edu). It is not our intent to replace the various e-conferences of e-conferences that are available. We want to provide a clearinghouse to feed e-conference announcements to all those maintaining the e-conferences and others who are interested.

> Send e-mail to listserv@listserv.nodak.edu with the message subscribe new-list Yourfirstname Yourlastname

NEW-LISTS

Contact: new-lists-request@mailbase.ac.uk

When a new list starts on the Mailbase system the details are posted to this list.

Send e-mail to mailbase@mailbase.ac.uk with the message subscribe new-lists Yourfirstname Yourlastname

NEWJOUR

Contact: Ann Okerson osap@cni.org—Jim O'Donnell jod@ccat.sas.upenn.edu

NewJour is the place to announce brand new or revised electronic networked academic, professional, research, scholarly, societal or topical electronic journals or newsletters. It is a place for messages that announce and describe briefly these new ventures in the early planning/announcement stages and/or at a more mature stage of actual development and availability. It is also the place to announce availability of paper journals and newsletters as they become available on - move into - electronic networks. Scholarly discussion lists which regularly and continuously maintain supporting files of substantive articles or preprints may also be reported; but this is not the outlet for reporting new lists or newspapers. newjour-digest is also available.

Send e-mail to majordomo@ccat.sas.upenn.edu with the message subscribe newjour Youremailaddress
Archives: http://gort.ucsd.edu/newjour

news.groups

Discussions and lists of newsgroups. The "official" forum for discussion of proposed new Usenet newsgroups.

Use a Usenet Newsreader to connect to news.groups
Archives: ftp://rtfm.mit.edu/news.groups/
ftp://rtfm.mit.edu/news.groups.questions/
ftp://rtfm.mit.edu/news.groups.reviews/

news.misc

Discussions of USENET itself.

Use a Usenet Newsreader to connect to news.misc
Archives: ftp://rtfm.mit.edu/news.misc/

NIS

Contact: Susan Calcari CALCARIS@CERF.NET

Network Information Services Announcements. Nis@cerf.net list will be a group effort (in true Internet style) to concentrate network information services (nis) announcements onto one list for everyone's use. A few dozen individuals around the Internet will each be monitoring a specific source (mailing list, news group, list

serv) and sending the information to CERFnet. We will serve as
the moderator, forwarding pertinent submissions to the entire read-
ership of the list, omitting duplicates. To volunteer to monitor a
source: send mail to nis@cerf.net. Sponsored by CERFnet.

Send e-mail to listserv@CERF.NET with the message subscribe
nis Yourfirstname Yourlastname

NNEWS

Contact Address: Dana Noonan noonan@msus1.msus.edu
Network News is an online newsletter focusing on library and information resources on the Internet. Updates information found
in _A Guide to Internet/Bitnet_.

Send e-mail to listserv@listserv.nodak.edu with the message subscribe nnews Yourfirstname Yourlastname or use a Usenet Newsreader to connect to bit.listserv.nnews

ONLINE-NEWS

Contact: Steve Outing owner-online-news@marketplace.com
ONLINE-NEWS is a list on the topic of online newspapers and
magazines. It will serve as a forum to discuss the evolution of newspaper and magazine experiments in electronic publishing.

Send e-mail to majordomo@marketplace.com with the message
subscribe online-news Youremailaddress

PCIP

Contact: pcip-request@list.nih.gov
Discussion group for the various sets of TCP/IP implementations
for personal computers. Bugs are reported here and help bringing
up a new environmment may be forthcoming from members of
this list. In the past, discussions have included the MIT package,
the Stanford TCP modifications and work at Wisconsin and Mary-
land.

Send e-mail to pcip-request@list.nih.gov or use a Usenet
Newsreader to connect to comp.protocols.tcp-ip.ibmpc

PERL-USERS

Contact: perl-users-request@ruby.oce.orst.edu
For discussion of PERL, Larry Wall's Practical Extraction and Report Language.

Send e-mail to PERL-USERS-REQUEST@ruby.oce.orst.edu or
use a Usenet Newsreader to connect to comp.lang.perl

POWER-PC
Contact: Harold Pritchett HAROLD@uga.cc.uga.edu
The POWER-PC list was created to discuss the new Apple/IBM/ Motorola PowerPC architecture processor line. Discussion can include personal RISC systems, technical workstations, notebook systems, and both midrange and high performance NIC systems based upon these processors.

> Send e-mail to listserv@uga.cc.uga.edu with the message subscribe power-pc Yourfirstname Yourlastname

PUBLIB-NET
Contact Address: publll@nysernet.org - John Iliff
iliffj@firnvx.firn.edu - Jean Armour Polly jpolly@nysernet.org
PUBLIB-NET is a discussion list concerned with use of the Internet in public libraries. Issues to be examined include connectivity, public access to the Internet, user and staff training, resources of interest to public librarians (online, print, video, other), electronic freedoms and responsibilities, new technologies for public library Internet access, National and regional public telecommunications policy and public libraries, and more.

> Send e-mail to listserv@nysernet.org with the message subscribe publib-net Yourfirstname Yourlastname
> Archives: gopher://gopher.nysernet.org

RFC
Contact: Jon Postel & Joyce Reynolds rfc-editor@isi.edu
Distribution of announcements of new Requests for Comments. These are the publications of the Internet protocol development community, and include the specifications of protocol standards for the Internet, as well as policy statements and informational memos.

> Send e-mail to RFC-DIST-REQUEST@ISI.EDU
> Archives: ftp://ds.internic.net/rfc

SOCSCI-WWW-GOPHER-NEWS-L
Contact: Dr. T. Matthew Ciolek tmciolek@coombs.anu.edu.au
The SocSci-WWW-Gopher-News-L forum was established to provide a world-wide communications/ notifications/ rapid announcements vehicle and a central electronic archive for anyone *building*, *maintaining* or *administering* the WWW and/or Gopher based information systems related to the broadly defined Social Sciences research, teaching and publications. When (as the sub-

scriber) you notify the forum about new WWW resources or interesting additions to the existing resources, please send your notices in the HTML format and written in the third person. Please test all the notices and attempt to keep them concise so that they could be added to the 'What's New in WWW Social Sciences' WWW Virtual Library page available from the URL http://coombs.anu.edu.au/WWWVLPages/WhatsNewWWW/socsci-www-news.html

Send e-mail to majordomo@coombs.anu.edu.au with the message subscribe socsci-www-gopher-news-l Youremailaddress

SOFTREVU
Contact: David B. O'Donnell atropos@aol.net
Forum for the Discussion of Small Computer Systems Software Reviews and Related Issues. SOFTREVU will provide a forum where users of personal computers and other small computing systems can review, discuss, and examine software products. Cross-platform compatibility issues related to software and hardware, with an emphasis placed on software, are also included in this forum. Subscribers are requested to keep personal vendettas off the list. This is not a forum for political or ethical discussions in any capacity; it is a forum for the discussion of software. Problems or complaints should be addressed to the list moderators. Anyone who does not maintain this policy, or is generally disruptive to the harmony of this list, will be removed.

Send e-mail to listserv@listserv.aol.com with the message subscribe softrevu Yourfirstname Yourlastname

SUPERK12
Contact: Carolyn A. Sprague richlist@ericir.syr.edu
High Performance Internet & Computer Apps in K-12 schools.

Send e-mail to SUPERK12–Request@listserv.syr.edu

TCP-IP
Contact: tcp-ip-request@nic.ddn.mil
Discussion of topics related to the TCP/IP protocols. It is hoped that this distribution list can aid in the following areas: To act as an on-line exchange among TCP developers and maintainers.—To announce new and expanded services in a timely manner.

Send e-mail to TCP-IP-REQUEST@NIC.DDN.MIL or majordomo@NIC.DDN.MIL with the message subscribe tcp-ip Yourfirstname Yourlastname or use a Usenet Newsreader to connect to comp.protocols.tcp-ip
Archives: ftp://nicfs.nic.ddn.mil/tcp-ip

UG-L

Usage Guidelines E-Conference is a discussion of the use and the abuse of the network; usage guidelines and etiquette; local access policies and enforcement of guidelines.

> Send e-mail to listserv@bitnic.educom.edu with the message subscribe ug-l Yourfirstname Yourlastname

VIRUS-L

Contact: Kenneth R. van Wyk krvw@assist.ims.disa.mil

Virus-L is a forum specifically for the discussion of computer virus experiences, protection software, and other virus related topics. The list is currently open to the public and is a digest format list (comp.virus is not digested). All VIRUS-L digests are archived and can be downloaded by any user.

> Send e-mail to listserv@LEHIGH.EDU with the message subscribe virus-l Yourfirstname Yourlastname or use a Usenet Newsreader to connect to comp.virus

WEB4LIB

Contact Address: Roy Tennant rtennant@library.berkeley.edu

WEB4LIB exists to foster discussion of issues relating to the creation and management of library-based World Wide Web servers and clients. Particularly appropriate issues for discussion include web resource selection, cataloging issues regarding web information, and in-house patron access to web servers.

> Send e-mail to listserv@library.berkeley.edu with the message subscribe web4lib Yourfirstname Yourlastname
> Archives: http://sunsite.berkeley.edu/Web4Lib/

WEBCRIT

Contact: Glenn Fleishman glenn@popco.com

The Web Critique mailing list is a spinoff of INET-MARKETING. Webcrit a discussion of your new Web sites, request critiques, and critique existing sites. This forum resulted from a high demand for such expression and critique.

> Send e-mail to listproc@popco.com with the message subscribe webcrit Yourfirstname Yourlastname

Web-Consultants

Contact: Al Silverberg alsil@just4u.com

The goal of web-consultants is to provide a Discussion List for those involved in Internet/Web consulting. This discussion list is open to all Internet /Web consultants.

> Send e-mail to web-consultants-request@just4u.com
>
> Archives: http://just4u.com/webconsultants/

Web/database Discussion Forum

Contact: j.p.rowe@larc.nasa.gov

This is a Web BBS. It is a good place to locate good Web programmers and get help and share your experiences.

> http://cscsun1.larc.nasa.gov/~beowulf/bbs/

Web-Support

Contact: mailbase-helpline@mailbase.ac.uk

For the discussion of issues relating to the World Wide Web, Web browsers (Mosaic and Cello in particular), Web servers (MacHTTP and serweb), the HTML language, HTML documents and editors, across Macintosh, DOS and Unix platforms in particular.

> Send e-mail to mailbase@mailbase.ac.uk with the message subscribe web-support Yourfirstname Yourlastname

WebWomen-HTML

Contact: donna.@niestu.com or donna2@niestu.com

The WebWomen-HTML list was formed to provide a space for women content providers on the web. Related topics might include advanced HTML, standards, design issues, graphics assistance, and even Java/Javascript. Newbies to the web are welcome; however, general newbie-to-Internet questions will be answered with pointers to FAQs.

> Send e-mail to webwomen-tech-request@niestu.com

WebWomen-Tech

Contact: donna.@niestu.com or donna2@niestu.com

The WebWomen-Tech list was formed to provide a space for technical women on the web. Related topics might include server modules, server configurations, CGI, Java, security issues, proxy servers, etc. It is an open and unmoderated list.

> Send e-mail to webwomen-tech-request@niestu.com

WINSOCK-L

Contact: Sam Bandak beast@mama.indstate.edu

Discussion list relating to Winsock related and based products. Virtually any topic related to Winsock, from the novice level to professional tips/advice, is germane. The Winsock-L list was created for users and developers of Winsock based, reliant and support applications to discuss any development and user configuration problems they might have about winsock applications. Winsock Development problems should be the major topic of this list. As a subscriber to this e-mail-based discussion list you will be able to access the list FTP site where you can download and upload different winsock based application (i.e. FTP, Mail, Archie, Gopher, Ping, Telnet, IRC, WEB, MOSAIC, Chat, Talk, and many other winsock based applications, etc.), and even games. This site is constantly being updated whenever a new freeware, shareware winsock software comes out, and you will always find the newest version of any winsock based applications. All of the newly uploaded software will take a day to be moved from the incoming directory to the appropriate directory, due to testing and virus checks.

Send e-mail to list-admin@papa.indstate.edu

Archives: ftp://papa.indstate.edu/winsock-l

WORKS

Contact: Dave Steiner WORKS-REQUEST@rutvm1.rutgers.edu
WorkS discusses personal work station computers, such as the Sun2, Sun3, Apollo, Silicon Graphics, and AT&T Workstations. WorkS provides a way for interested members of the Internet community to discuss what is wrong with these machines, compare notes on work in progress, and share useful insights about these kinds of systems.

Send e-mail to listserv@rutvm1.rutgers.edu with the message subscribe works Yourfirstname Yourlastname

WWW-CIS

Contact: Stefano Bonacina stefano_bonacina@sgs-thomson.it
Discussion of topics related to the use and implementation of WWW for Corporate Information Systems. Corporate Information providers could put internal documents available only to the internal community making possible for every user with a TCP/IP connection and a WWW browser to use just one tool to access several types of data, such as employee telephone number and office address, or search for all employees at a location or something like that without having to learn new or different query tools.

Send e-mail to majordomo@sgs-thomson.it with the message subscribe www-cis Yourfirstname Yourlastname

www-sites
Commercial sites have their own issues with using World Wide Web technology. Companies' concerns range from liability when using free software and finding solid or simply commercial solutions through deciding how to deploy an infrastructure. This list is for discussion of these issues, and for sharing solutions that have worked.

    Send e-mail to majordomo@qiclab.scn.rain.com with the message subscribe www-sites Youremailaddress

WWW-VM
Discussion of World Wide Web for IBM/VM systems.

    Subscription Information: listserv@sjuvm.stjohns.edu with the message subscribe www-vm Yourfirstname Yourlastname

Appendix E

Bibliography for IIPOPs

This bibliography is not meant to be comprehensive. Entries were selected because we have found them helpful in learning how to be an Internet Information Producer or Provider. Some entries are not annotated because the title speaks for itself.

BASIC INTERNET CONNECTIONS INFORMATION

Dowd, Kevin. *Getting Connected: The Internet at 56K and Up*. Sebastopol, Calif.: O'Reilly & Associates, 1996.
This book is outstanding information for people making decisions to establish higher speed Internet connections at their site.

Engst, Adam C. *The Internet Starter Kit for Macintosh*. Indianapolis, Ind.: Hayden Books, 1995.
Engst discusses PPP, SLIP, and TCP/IP software for connecting Macintosh or Microsoft Windows microcomputers to the Internet. He also compares and contrasts commercial, public-access Internet providers on their cost for dial-up shell, PPP, SLIP, and dedicated-line connections.

Estrada, Susan. *Connecting to the Internet: A Buyer's Guide*. Sebastopol, Calif.: O'Reilly & Associates, 1993.
Estrada gives the nontechnical person who must make decisions about Internet access a marvelous system for evaluating the type

of access needed. This is our favorite source for detailed information about how different Internet access mechanisms work and what level of access they will provide. Estrada provides details about hardware, software, and personnel requirements for the different access options as well.

Schneider, Karen. *The Internet Access Cookbook*. New York: Neal-Schuman Publishers, 1996.

GENERAL INTERNET

Benson, Allen. *Internet Companion for Librarians*. New York: Neal-Schuman Publishers, 1995.

Hahn, Harley. *The Internet Complete Reference*, 2d ed. Berkeley, Calif.: Osborne McGraw-Hill, 1996.

John, Nancy Regina, and Edward J. Valauskas. *The Internet Troubleshooter: Help for the Logged-on and Lost*. Chicago: American Library Association, 1994.
This book explains and offers solutions to the variety of error messages, connection problems and arcane computer messages that are frequently encountered on the Internet.

Liu, Cricket, Jerry Peck, Russ Jones, Bryan Buus, and Adrian Nye. *Managing Internet Information Services*. Sebastopol, Calif.: O'Reilly & Associates, 1994.
This book is required reading for those who will be working with network consultants to assist learners in setting up and running Internet services including mailers, FTP sites, telnet sites, Gopher, and World Wide Web servers. We have recommended this book to the systems administrators at sites where we have provided training.

SECURITY ISSUES

Chapman, Brent, and Elizabeth Zwicky. *Building Internet Firewalls*. Sebastopol, Calif.: O'Reilly & Associates, 1996.

Cheswick, William R., and Steven M. Bellovin. *Firewalls and Internet Security: Repelling the Wily Hacker.* Reading, Mass.: Addison-Wesley, 1994.

This book is essential for anyone responsible for network security. It discusses what kinds of Firewalls there are, how to build a Firewall, and how to test it.

Garfinkel, Simson. *PGP: Pretty Good Privacy.* Sebastopol, Calif.: O'Reilly & Associates, 1995.

This book describes itself as "encryption for everyone." This is an informed and thorough discussion of encryption as a way of maintaining privacy for information transmitted across the Internet. PGP is one popular and easily implemented tool for encryption.

Sterling, Bruce. *The Hacker Crackdown.* New York: Bantam, 1993.

Entertaining and enlightening discussion of computer crime from the point of view of the telephone companies, federal law enforcement, and the "criminals" themselves.

TCP/IP NETWORKING AND INTERNET NETWORK ADMINISTRATION

Albitz, Paul, and Cricket Liu. *DNS and BIND.* Sebastopol, Calif.: O'Reilly & Associates, 1994.

Essential guide to the Domain Name System and the Berkeley Internet Name Domain implementation for Unix. This book provides information that network managers will need to maintain a domain name server.

Comer, Douglas. *Internetworking with TCP/IP: Principles, Protocols, and Architecture.* Englewood Cliffs, N.J.: Prentice Hall, 1988.

Eckel, George. *Building a Linux Internet Server.* New York: Prentice Hall, 1996.

Eckel, George. *Building a UNIX Internet Server.* Indianapolis, Ind.: New Riders, 1996.

Eckel, George. *Building a Windows NT Internet Server.* Indianapolis, Ind.: New Riders, 1996.

Frey, Donnalyn, and Rick Adams. *!%@:: A Directory of Electronic Mail Addressing and Networks*. 4th ed. Sebastopol, Calif.: O'Reilly and Associates, 1994.
This book is intended for systems administrators or network managers who are running mailers with TCP/IP networks.

Hunt, Craig. *TCP/IP Network Administration*. Sebastopol, Calif.: O'Reilly & Associates, 1994.
Detailed guide for TCP/IP network administration on the Unix operating system.

Hunt, Craig. *Networking Personal Computers with TCP/IP*. Sebastopol, Calif.: O'Reilly & Associates, 1996.
Detailed guide for TCP/IP networking of Windows, Windows 95, and Windows NT microcomputers.

Kirch, Olaf. *Linux Network Adminstrator's Guide*. [self-published] Darmstadt, Germany: Olaf Kirch, Kattreinstr. 38, 64295 (okir@monad.swb.de)

Steadman, Carl, and Jason Snell. *Providing Internet Services via the Mac OS*. New York: Addison-Wesley, 1996.

INTERNET TRAINING

Kovacs, Diane. *The Internet Trainer's Guide*. New York: Van Nostrand Reinhold, 1995.

WORLD WIDE WEB APPLICATIONS

December, John, and Neil Randall. *The World Wide Web Unleashed: Everything You Need to Master the Web*. Indianapolis, Ind.: Sams Publishing, 1994.
This book contains technical details about the World Wide Web servers and clients available as well as a tutorial on HTML and homepage design. It is a little out of date right now, but December maintains a homepage with updated information on it.

Flanagan, David. *Java in a Nutshell*. Sebastopol, Calif.:

O'Reilly & Associates, 1996.

Gundavaram, Shishir. *CGI Programming*. Sebastopol, Calif.: O'Reilly & Associates, 1996.

Musciano, Chuck and Bill Kennedy. *HTML: The Definitive Guide*. Sebastopol, Calif.: O'Reilly & Associates, 1996.

Rowe, Jeff. *Building Internet Database Servers/CGI*. Indianapolis, Ind.: New Riders, 1996.
This is a Webmaster's guide to Internet database servers. It guides readers through the process of putting their database on the Internet and outlines the procedures involved in Internet commerce.

World Wide Web Journal: Fourth International World Wide Web Conference Proceedings, December 11–14, 1995, Boston, Massachusetts. Sebastopol, Calif.: O'Reilly & Associates, 1995.

PUBLICATIONS BY CASE DESCRIPTION CONTACTS

Bailey, Charles W., Jr. "Electronic (Online) Publishing in Action: The Public-Access Computer Systems Review and Other Electronic Serials." *Online* 15 (January 1991): 28–35.

Bailey, Charles W., Jr. "The Public-Access Computer Systems Review: A Network-Based Electronic Journal." In *The Public-Access Computer Systems Review*. Vol. 1, 1990. Edited by Charles W. Bailey, Jr., Leslie B. Pearse, and Michael Ridley, vii–x. Chicago: Library and Information Technology Association, 1992.

Directory of Electronic Journals, Newsletters and Academic Discussion Lists. 6th ed. Washington, D.C.: Association of Research Libraries, 1996.
Academic discussion lists part is available as the *Directory of Scholarly and Professional Electronic Conferences*, Diane K. Kovacs, Editor-in-Chief, http://www.n2h2.com/KOVACS.

JOURNAL ARTICLES AND ISSUES

***Byte*, March 1996.**
Articles on the key technologies for establishing a Web site using microcomputers. Also articles on VRML and Web page design.

***Internet World*, April 1996.**
Articles on how to build a Web Site on a budget and much more. Includes reviews of HTML editing programs.

***Network Computing*, May 1, 1996.**
Reviews of 5 Internet servers with Web server capabilities, 11 Web browsers, and 6 TCP/IP suites. All of these are very high-level commercial packages. The article includes prices.

Index*

---

*The following typographical conventions are used in the index: **Boldface** identifies material contained in the Appendix section of the book; *Italic* page numbers indicate material contained in the preface.

Colophon

Diane K. Kovacs is President of Kovacs Consulting—Internet & World Wide Web Training & Consulting. She has more than six years of experience as an Internet Trainer and Consultant.

Diane's first book *The Internet Trainer's Guide*, was published by Van Nostrand Reinhold in 1995. Another book, *The Internet Training Tool Kit*, is forthcoming from Von Nostrand Reinhold in 1997.

Diane is the editor-in-chief of *The Directory of Scholarly and Professional Electronic Conferences* (published in print by the Association of Research Libraries) and of the *Electronic Journal on Virtual Culture*, a peer-reviewed electronic journal.

She was the recipient of the Apple Corporation Library's Internet Citizen Award for 1992 and was the University of Illinois Graduate School of Library and Information Science Alumni Association's first recipient of the Young Leadership Award in 1996.

Diane received an M.S. in Library and Information Science from the University of Illinois in 1989 and an M.Ed in Instructional Technology from Kent State University in 1993.

Michael J. Kovacs is a Project Manager for Mega Solutions, Inc., a Cleveland, Ohio based computer and network consulting firm. He has nearly ten years of experience in Internet and other networking and systems administration on UNIX computer systems. Michael specializes in Internet security, World Wide Web site administration, and developing secure CGI BIN applications for corporate Intranets.

He is the Listowner for ACM-L - Discussion of and for the Association for Computing Machinery.

Michael holds a Bachelor of Science degree in Computer Science from Kent State University.

Additional Titles of Interest

THE INTERNET SEARCHER'S HANDBOOK
Locating Information, People, and Software

By Peter Morville, Louis B. Rosenfeld, and Joseph Janes

Ideal for reference librarians, students, and researchers, this practical, step-by-step guide is a current tutorial for resource discovery on the Internet. It helps novice or advanced Internet users conduct research investigations—and find answers to quick reference queries. The handbook provides in-depth coverage on all useful and usable resources, including virtual libraries, Internet directories, communities of people, and Internet search tools. An example of a real search is given for each resource. Ways to streamline locating information—and addresses and instructions for a broad but selective list of Internet subject guides, directories and search engines—are also offered. Additional sections include a review of other types of information resources, such as electronic discussion lists and conferencing tools.

1-55570-236-8. 1996. 6 x 9. 236 pp. $35.00.

"From simple reference questions to more complex research . . . this guide shows how to use various Internet tools and resources to extract the data." *Library Journal*

USING THE WORLD WIDE WEB AND CREATING HOME PAGES:
A How-To-Do-It Manual for Librarians

By Ray E. Metz and Gail Junion-Metz

This guide gives you all the information you need to browse the Web, integrate it into your library services, and build an attractive and functional home page for your library. Using easy to follow, step-by-step instructions, the manual covers hardware and software requirements; choosing and using a Web browser; and training library staff and patrons to use the Web. The book also shows how to use the Web to expand sources available at the reference desk; find the best resources for children; bring in multimedia resources; archive information; and assist with library operations and services like interlibrary loan, cataloging, and foreign language collections. Special sections also detail how to create HTML documents and design a home page for your library or department.

1-55570-241-4. 1996. 8 1/2 x 11. 290 pp. $49.95.

"Virtually jargon-free . . . Highly recommended." *Library Journal*

"Written in accessible language with easy-to-follow instructions . . . an excellent addition to the professional shelf." *Curriculum Administrator*

TECHNOLOGY AND COPYRIGHT LAW:
A Guidebook for the Library, Research, and Teaching Professions

By Arlene Bielefeld and Lawrence Cheesemen

This groundbreaking guide to technology copyright issues—designed and written for non-lawyers—will help you anticipate, avoid, and respond appropriately to legal difficulties stemming from electronic copyright. Part I covers historical and legal background, and also looks at trends for the future, including the probable effects of recommendations from the National Information Infrastructure Report. Part II explores technology and copyright in libraries and classrooms, focusing on fair use doctrine, broadcasting, duplication and distribution, first sale doctrine, and contractual agreements. Part III offers information on copyright law and the electronic classroom, networks, and international agreements. The guide concludes with topical checklists, model policies and remedies, plus an index and appendixes including copyright guidelines from ALA and the Committee on New Technological Uses.

1-55570-267-8. 1997. 6 x 9. 213 pp. $49.95.

To order or request further information, contact:
Neal-Schuman Publishers
100 Varick Street, New York NY 10013
212-925-8650
or fax toll free—1-800-584-2414